Business Concepts
for English Practice

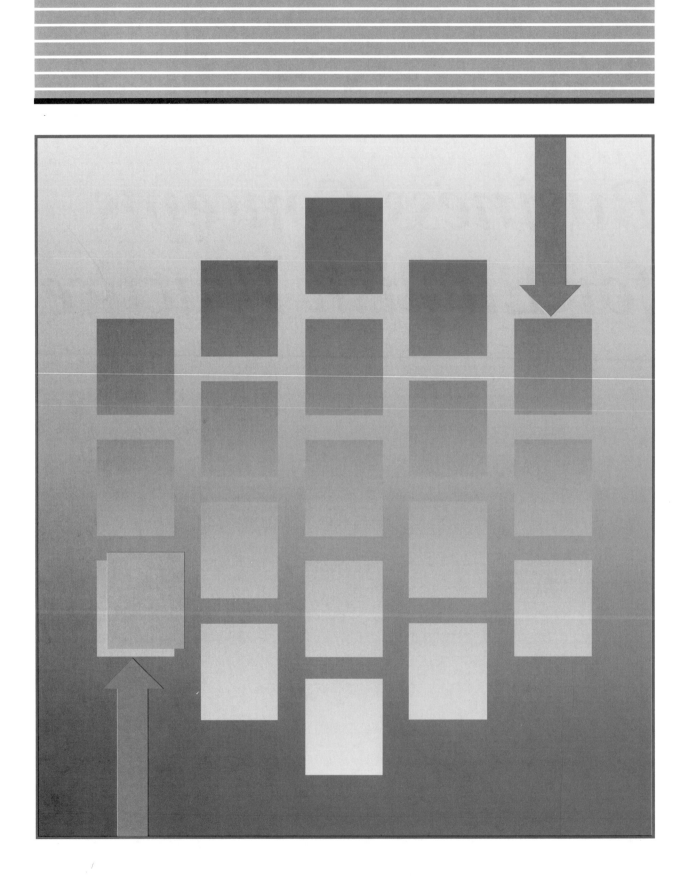

Business Concepts
for English Practice

SECOND EDITION

Barbara Tolley Dowling
OREGON STATE UNIVERSITY

Marianne McDougal Arden

HEINLE & HEINLE PUBLISHERS
A Division of Wadsworth, Inc.
Boston, Massachusetts 02116   U.S.A.

Publisher: Stanley J. Galek
Editor: Erik Gundersen
Associate Editor: Lynne Telson Barsky
Editorial Production Manager: Elizabeth Holthaus
Production Editor: Kristin M. Thalheimer
Photo Coordinator: Martha Leibs-Heckly
Manufacturing Coordinator: Jerry Christopher
Project Manager: Anne Benaquist
Part Opener Art Design: Nancy Lindgren
Interior Design: Rita Naughton
Cover Design: Bortman Design Group/Howie Green

Library of Congress Cataloging–in–Publication Data

Dowling, Barbara Tolley.
    Business concepts for English practice / Barbara Tolley Dowling,
Marianne McDougal Arden. — 2nd ed.

    p.   cm.

    Rev. ed. of Business concepts for English practice. 1982.

    ISBN 0–8384–4077–0

    1. Readers—Business.   2. English language—Textbooks for foreign speakers.   3. Business—Problems,
exercises, etc.   4. English language—Business English.   I. Dowling, Barbara Tolley. Business concepts
for English practice.   II. Title.
PE1127.B86D69   1992
428.2'4'02465—dc20   92–31120
                                                                              CIP

Photo Credits: Apple Computers 158; Comstock 2, 10, 46, 54, 112, 143; Geer/Mink (Tony Stone
Worldwide/Chicago Ltd.) 167, Joseph Pobereskin (Tony Stone Worldwide) 134; Michael Lajoie 34, 68, 76,
88, 96, 122; John Coletti (Stock Boston) 26

Manufactured in the United States of America

Heinle & Heinle Publishers is a division of Wadsworth, Inc.

10   9

To Chuck, Tom, Patrick, and Hillary

Contents

I. INTRODUCTION   1

1. Business Basics   2

1.1 What is Business?   2
1.2 Careers in Business   10
1.3 Choosing a Career   20

II. THE GLOBAL MARKETPLACE   25

2. Marketing   26

2.1 The Four P's   26
2.2 The Target Market   34
2.3 Market Research and Product Design   43

3. International Business   46

3.1 Why Nations Trade   46
3.2 Multinational Corporations   54
3.3 Exploring Foreign Markets: Customs and Cultures   63

III. FINANCIAL ASPECTS OF BUSINESS OPERATIONS   67

4. Accounting   68

4.1 An Accounting Overview   68
4.2 The Balance Sheet   76
4.3 Preparing an Income Statement   85

5. Finance   88

5.1 Why Finance?   88
5.2 Acquisition of Capital   96
5.3 Acquiring Start-up Capital for a Small Business   105

IV. HUMAN ASPECTS OF BUSINESS ORGANIZATIONS   111

6. Management   112

6.1 Management Functions   112
6.2 Management and Human Resources Development   122
6.3 Looking at Leadership Styles   130

7. Decision Making 134

   7.1 Steps in the Decision Process 134
   7.2 The Reality of Decision Making 143
   7.3 Deciding Who Decides 153

V. BUSINESS AND TECHNOLOGY 157

8. Computer Applications 158

   8.1 Business Computer Systems 158
   8.2 Expert Systems 167
   8.3 Solving a "Stock Out" Problem 175

APPENDICES 179

A. Management 6.3: Looking at Leadership Styles 180

B. Computer Applications 8.3: Solving a "Stock Out" Problem 181

C. One Man's Model for Case Analysis 184

D. Case Studies 186

GLOSSARY 191

To the Teacher

In the ten years since *Business Concepts for English Practice* was first published there have been dramatic changes in the business environment and continuing evolution in language teaching methodology. This second edition reflects these most recent developments and is designed to be a more effective, up-to-date teaching/learning tool. This edition includes the following features:

- completely new computer technology unit, focusing on business applications and expert systems
- new task-based, integrated activities based on real-life business situations
- updated readings, graphs and charts, and supplementary activities
- revised exercises, especially writing tasks
- appendices, including business cases and guidelines on the case study method

This book is a business-oriented English text with both an academic and an applied focus. It is intended for intermediate to advanced students of English who have an academic and/or professional interest in business. For students with little or no business background, basic concepts are explained and developed in the readings, and terms are defined in the glossary. Those with experience in the business world and advanced language proficiency will be able to move more quickly through the readings and on to the application exercises and task-based activities.

Purpose

The primary goal of *Business Concepts for English Practice* is to provide language practice based on subject-specific readings in such areas as marketing, international business, management, and computer applications. The business concepts included in these readings serve as springboards for activities in text analysis, classification, writing, information transfer, and the contextualization and development of vocabulary. The main objectives of the text are as follows:

- to develop reading skills and provide practice in comprehending written business discourse
- to present technical and subtechnical business vocabulary through contextualization at both the sentence and the paragraph levels
- to present high-interest, interactive situations based on actual business applications
- to provide activities for practice and improvement of general language skills and critical thinking

Description

The student book has five units, followed by appendices and a glossary. In addition to the introductory unit, entitled "Business Basics", the other units cover seven functional areas of business: Unit II, "Marketing and International Business"; Unit III,

"Accounting and Finance"; Unit IV, "Management and Decision Making", and Unit V, "Computer Applications." These areas were selected because they form the core subjects of introductory business textbooks used in academic programs. Each chapter has three parts: (1) a subject-specific reading and exercises; (2) another reading from the same content area and exercises; and (3) a task-based, interactive activity. The text concludes with appendices (including additional cases and information about case study analysis) and a glossary in which technical, subtechnical, and general English terms from the chapter vocabulary lists are defined.

Classroom Application

Business Concepts for English Practice can be used as the core text in an English for Business and Economics "special program" or in an ESP (English for Specific Purposes) business reading course. It can be utilized as a supplementary text in a business application/communication course, in an ESP business writing course, or in a general English reading and vocabulary course.

While *Business Concepts for English Practice* has been written for non-native speakers of English, it could also be used for native speakers in high school or community college developmental reading programs, in either a classroom or tutorial situation. In a prebusiness program, this text might be used to introduce students to basic concepts they will encounter in their business courses.

Seven-to-ten class hours are required to complete each chapter. The amount of time needed depends on such variables as the number of exercises used, the quantity of outside work given, and the language proficiency of the students.

The chapters are sequenced so that business content increases in difficulty. "Business Basics" introduces the format of the text and is conceptually and linguistically easier than subsequent chapters. This chapter allows for assessment of student language proficiency and business interests.

After completion of the introductory chapter, the remaining chapters may be used in sequence, or subject areas may be selected based on class interests. Because exercises are spiraled throughout the text, if chapters are taken out of order, it may be necessary to refer to the place where the linguistic feature or activity was first introduced in order to present whatever background information the students may need to complete the exercise (e.g., definition forms and explanation of classification).

Subject-Specific Readings

The two readings in each chapter present aspects of the subject matter normally included in introductory business texts. The initial reading provides an overview of the business area; the second reading concentrates on a more specific topic. For example, the marketing chapter includes an overview of the field, followed by a detailed exploration of one aspect of marketing, the target market. An effort has been made to use the different rhetorical modes that are typically found in business textbooks—e.g., definition, comparison and contrast, cause and effect, and classification.

Exercises

The language practice and business application exercises following the readings focus on understanding the texts and the technical and subtechnical terms used. In addition, these exercises associate and integrate other skills—especially oral communication, writing, and study skills. The application, classification, and information transfer exercises provide opportunities for language practice in applying the business concepts presented in the readings. In each chapter the activities are organized and sequenced as follows:

Prereading Activity*	Vocabulary Exercises*	Writing
Vocabulary*	Text Analysis*	Information Transfer
Comprehension*	Classification	Additional Activities
	Application	

Business Tasks

The third part of each chapter is a culminating, task-based activity in which students integrate concepts studied in the chapter as well as a range and variety of language skills. A business roleplay, simulation, or case study forms the core of each activity, and students are given the opportunity to participate actively in real-life business situations.

Gradation of Exercises

The exercises are presented at different levels of difficulty to offer language practice for students with intermediate to advanced English proficiency. A wide range of activities at various levels provides a mechanism for working with groups of mixed language abilities, which is often necessary in English for Specific Purposes courses.

Beginning with the comprehension sections, each exercise is preceded by a proficiency marker. These markers are intended as a general guide:

★ intermediate
★★ upper intermediate
★★★ advanced

When a marker is placed before a question, it refers to that question and all subsequent ones until the next marker appears. Although the proficiency markers are designed to give an approximation of the language proficiency a student needs to complete the task, business experience and training of the individual are also factors, especially for the most advanced exercises, which sometimes require some business background as well as advanced language proficiency.

Supplementary Materials

A teacher's manual provides additional information on the business and linguistic aspects explored in the student book, *Business Concepts for English Practice*. The manual contains detailed descriptions of the exercises and their objectives, notes on methodology and classroom application, and an answer key.

Acknowledgments

We wish to acknowledge the English Language Institute, Oregon State University, for its unfailing cooperation on this project, especially in the first edition. We sincerely appreciate the professional and moral support we received from the ELI staff. In writing this second edition, we credit Helen Polensek with the theoretical framework used as the basis for the task-based business activities in the third part of each chapter.

We thank the following people for their review of the material for technical accuracy: Tom Dowling, Deborah Healey, Tom Owen, Bill Patton, Barbara Rose, Eve Sanchez, Roberto Sanchez, Jeanne Soth, Brian Soth, and Bruce Osen.

We also wish to acknowledge the instructors who field-tested the materials: Paul Barker, Warner Pacific College; James Baxter and R.M. Pehlke, Procter and Gamble; Tom Cope and Eve Sanchez, Oregon State University; and Kim Lee, College of Marin.

---

*These activities appear in both the first and second parts of each unit. Those that are not starred occur in only one section of each chapter.

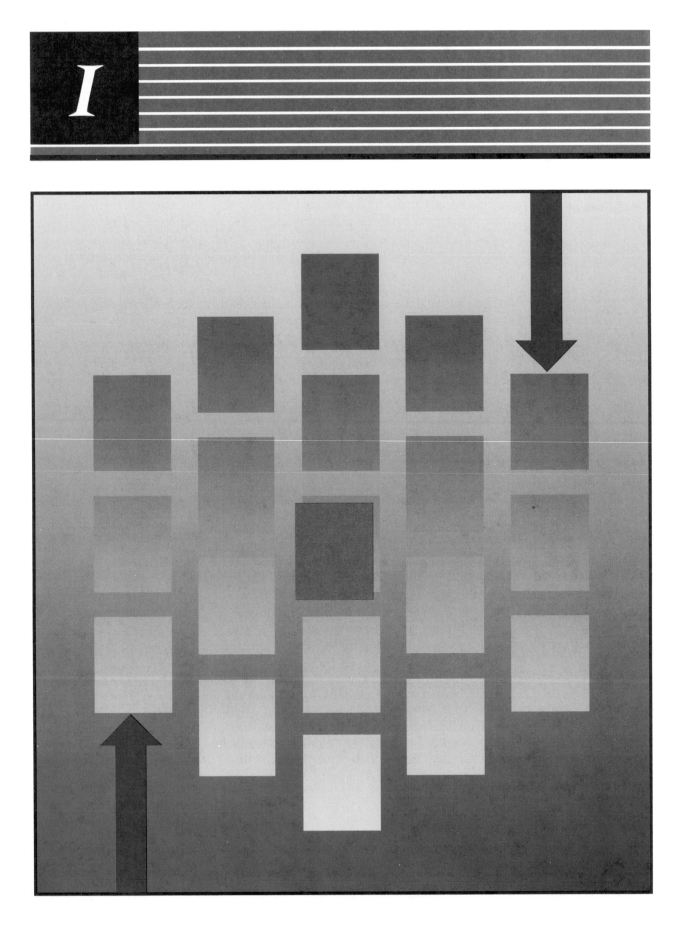

Introduction

1. Business Basics

1.1 What Is Business?

1.2 Careers in Business

1.3 Choosing a Career

1. Business Basics

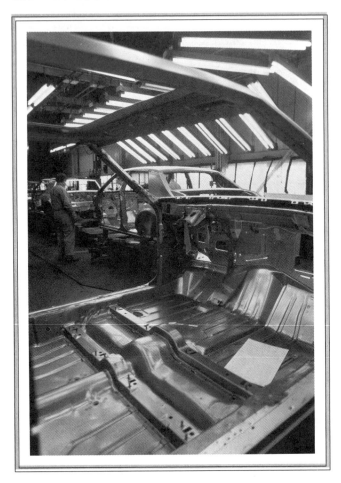

Business Basics 1.1: WHAT IS BUSINESS?

Prereading Activity

Discuss the following questions.

1. When you see the word *business*, what do you think about? Quickly write down words or ideas as they come into your mind.

   seller, customer, money

   _____

   _____

   Now discuss your notes with your classmates.

2. Write your own definition of business in the space provided below. Begin your definition in this way:

   Business is _____

   _____

   _____

   Compare your definition with the one written by the person next to you. Add to your definition if you find any new information.

Vocabulary

Below is a list of terms that you will find in the text. As you read "What Is Business?," see if you understand each term. Use this as a working list and add other terms that you do not know.

NOUNS	VERBS	ADJECTIVES	OTHERS
exchange	examine	technical	for instance
production	classify	various	on the other hand
distribution	perform	_____	_____
sale	remain	_____	_____
goods	create	_____	_____
services	_____		
profit	_____		
conversion	_____		
surplus			
expenses			
_____			
_____			
_____			

Reading

WHAT IS BUSINESS?

Business is a word that is commonly used in many different languages. But exactly what does it mean? The concepts and activities of business have increased in modern times. Traditionally, business simply meant exchange or trade for things people wanted or needed. Today it has a more technical definition. One

5 definition of business is the production, distribution, and sale of goods and services for a profit. To examine this definition, we will look at its various parts.

First, production is the creation of services or the changing of materials into products. One example is the conversion of iron ore into metal car parts. Next, these products need to be moved from the factory to the marketplace. This is

10 known as distribution. A car might be moved from a factory in Detroit to a car dealership in Miami.

Third is the sale of goods and services. Sale is the exchange of a product or service for money. A car is sold to someone in exchange for money. Goods are products that people either need or want; for example, cars can be classified as

15 goods. Services, on the other hand, are activities that a person or group performs for another person or organization. For instance, an auto mechanic performs a service when he repairs a car. A doctor also performs a service by taking care of people when they are sick.

Business, then, is a combination of all these activities: production, distribu-

20 tion, and sale. However, there is one other important factor. This factor is the creation of profit or economic surplus. A major goal in the functioning of an American business company is making a profit. Profit is the money that remains after all the expenses are paid. Creating an economic surplus or profit is, therefore, a primary goal of business activity.

Comprehension

⭐ **A.** Answer the following questions about the meaning of business. Questions with asterisks (*) cannot be answered directly from the text.

1. What is one modern definition of business?
2. *How does this modern meaning of business differ from the traditional one? *What factors have brought about these changes?
3. What does production involve?
4. What example of distribution is given in the reading? *Can you think of another example?
5. How do goods differ from services?
6. In addition to production, distribution, and sale, what other factor is important in defining business?
7. What is profit? *In general, what do companies do with their profits?
8. Compare your definition of business with the one given in the reading. *How are they similar? *In what ways does your definition differ from the one presented in the text?

★★ **B.** Determine which of the following statements are *true* and which are *false*. Then put *T* or *F* in the blanks. Rewrite false statements to make them true.

1. __*T*__ Business is not just one activity but a combination of different operations, such as production, distribution, and sale.

2. _____ From ancient to modern times the definition of business has remained the same.

3. _____ Moving a truckload of oranges from the orchard to the supermarket is an example of production.

4. _____ A salesclerk provides a service by answering customers' questions.

Vocabulary Exercises

★★ **A.** Write down any terms that you did not understand in the reading. Find each term in the reading, look at its context, and try to figure out the meaning. Discuss these terms with your classmates.

★ **B.** Look at the terms in the left-hand column and find the correct synonyms in the right-hand column. Copy the corresponding letters in the blanks.

1. __*g*__ goods (line 5)   a. moving or transporting

2. _____ conversion (line 8)   b. trade

3. _____ for instance (line 16)   c. however

4. _____ distribution (line 10)   d. look at

5. _____ exchange (line 12)   e. change

6. _____ on the other hand (line 15)   f. for example

7. _____ examine (line 6)   ✔ g. products

★ **C.** Complete the sentences with the noun and verb forms provided.

1. **sales/sells**

   a. An annual report includes the ___*sales*___ figures of the company for the current fiscal year.

   b. An auto dealership ___*sells*___ cars, trucks, vans, and sometimes recreational vehicles.

2. **distribution/distribute**

   a. Some companies hold exclusive _____ rights for specific products.

   b. Factory representatives _____ products to wholesalers and retailers.

3. **production/produces**

   a. How efficiently a company _____ its products will in large measure determine its success.

   b. The _____ of high-technology instruments is one of the most rapidly growing industries in the 1990s.

4. **classification/are classified**

    a. Items _____ in order to show the relationship between them.

    b. _____ means the grouping of items to show the differences between them.

5. **conversion/convert**

    a. When traveling from country to country, people _____ one currency to another.

    b. The production process often involves the _____ of raw materials into finished products.

Text Analysis

★   **Look at the reading to answer these questions.**

1. The reading contains terms such as *its, it,* and *this factor*. These terms refer to nouns or noun phrases that occurred earlier in the text. For example, *its* in line 6 refers to *one definition of business* in lines 4–5. What does each of the following refer to?

LINES	WORDS	REFERENTS
4	it	_____
20	this factor	_____

2. Transition words or phrases are used to clarify the relationships between sentences. They are usually placed at the beginning of new ideas. Transitions can be divided into groups according to their functions. Match the following.

    _____ next (line 8)   a. summarizing

    _____ on the other hand (line 15)   b. sequencing information

    _____ therefore (lines 23–24)   c. contrasting

3. Line 8 refers to *its various parts*. List the parts of the business definition that are explained in the reading.

    a. *production* _____

    b. _____

    c. _____

    d. _____

4. What key transition words are used to introduce each new part of the definition?

TRANSITION WORDS		PARTS OF THE DEFINITION
a. *first*	→	*production*
b. _____	→	_____
c. _____	→	_____
d. _____	→	_____

5. A definition may take this form:

Production   →   is   →   the changing of materials into products
                                        or the creation of services

term being defined   →   verb *to be*   →   definition

A number of terms are defined this way in the reading. Find and copy these definitions in the spaces below.

a. *Business is* _____

_____

b. _____

_____

c. _____

_____

d. _____

_____

e. _____

_____

Classification

★★   Classification means the grouping of items to show the relationship between them. Items that are classified together have something in common; that is, something must apply to all the items in that group or class. Look at the items below. They may be classified as either goods or services. Review the definitions and examples given in the reading (lines 13–18). Classify the following items as either goods or services.

✔ 1. car
✔ 2. medical diagnosis
  3. travel agency
  4. briefcase
  5. auto repair
  6. financial planning
  7. computer

  8. video cassette recorder
  9. management consulting
 10. accounting ledger
 11. calculator
 12. job placement
 13. suit
 14. forklift

 15. office equipment repair
 16. newspaper delivery
 17. computer programming
 18. time clock
 19. law book
 20. income tax preparation

GOODS	SERVICES
car	*medical diagnosis*

Application

★★★   **A.** Match these parts of the business definition to the following real-life situations.

- production of goods
- distribution of goods
- sale of goods
- sale of services

Examples:

Iron ore is made into metal car parts.   *production of goods*

A car is moved from a factory to a car dealership.   *distribution of goods*

A salesperson sells a car.   *sale of goods*

An auto mechanic repairs a car.   *sale of services*

1. A shipment of grain is transferred from a boat to a truck. _____

2. A chemical plant turns raw materials into fertilizer. _____

3. A salesperson from a concrete manufacturer convinces the owner of a building materials company to buy a shipment of drainage pipe from his company. _____

4. A warehouse ships books to a bookstore. _____

5. A computer manufacturer receives silicon chips and puts them into minicomputers. _____

6. A dentist repairs a child's broken tooth. _____

7. A train moves truck parts across the country. _____

8. A grocer exchanges groceries for money. _____

9. A waitress takes your order for lunch. _____

10. A farmer plants vegetables for harvest in the fall. _____

★★★   **B.** With your partner, write down real-life situations that would fit into the categories of production, distribution, and sale. For examples, see the preceding exercise.

production: _____

_____

_____

distribution: _____

_____

_____

sale: _____

_____

Writing

★★★   Write a paragraph about a business operation with which you are familiar. Include the categories of production, distribution, and sale in your description.

Example:

From the initial drilling for oil to the final sale of gasoline at the pump, oil passes through a variety of stages. After the oil has been taken from the ground, it is refined into gasoline during the production process. Then the gasoline is taken from the refinery and shipped by either truck or rail. It is sold to wholesalers who distribute it, or it is directly distributed by the company to the gas stations. Finally, the gasoline is purchased by customers who need it for their cars, trucks, or other vehicles.

Additional Activities

1. Ask a business professional to give you a definition of business. Then ask someone who does not work in business to give you a definition. Compare the results.
2. Create a questionnaire and interview someone from a local business about the areas of production, distribution, and sale as they relate to that particular enterprise.
3. Use the Apple computer program entitled "Business Organization" (also available in filmstrips), Social Studies School Service, 10200 Jefferson Blvd., P.O. Box 802, Culver City, CA 90232-0802.

Business Basics: 1.2: CAREERS IN BUSINESS

Prereading Activity

Discuss the following questions.

1. Have you ever had a job? Describe your most interesting one. How did you get it? What training or skills were required? What kinds of duties did you perform?

2. Name some of the different fields of business in which a person may work, such as marketing. Then list some of the specializations within the different fields. For example, within marketing one may specialize in advertising or selling.

marketing _____ → *advertising, selling,* _____

_____ → _____

_____ → _____

_____ → _____

3. Before selecting a career (the chosen work of one's life), what should a person try to find out about himself or herself and the job?

_____

_____

_____

_____

_____

_____

_____

_____

_____

_____

Vocabulary

Below is a list of terms that you will find in the text. As you read "Careers in Business," see if you understand each term. Use this as a working list and add other terms that you do not know.

NOUNS	VERBS	ADJECTIVES	OTHERS
career	offer	suitable	consequently
variety	specialize in	available	
field			
salary			
aptitude			
demand			
advancement			

Reading

CAREERS IN BUSINESS

Business is an increasingly important activity throughout the world today. Consequently, the opportunities for a business career have grown in variety and number. There are now five broad fields, or areas, of business that offer exciting careers:

5

- management
- marketing
- accounting
- finance
- computers and data processing

10

Within each of these fields are specific jobs in which you can specialize. For example, within the field of marketing you can specialize in market research, advertising, buying, selling, or distribution. The figure below shows general career opportunities that are available in the various fields of business.

Figure 1

15

In choosing a business career, there are several questions you may want to ask. For instance, does the work interest you? Are there any areas of business for which you have an aptitude or special capability? What are the opportunities involved, such as salary, chance for advancement, and demand (or need) for the job? Answers to these kinds of questions and careful planning will help you choose a suitable and successful career in business.

Comprehension

A. Answer the following questions about business careers. Questions with asterisks (*) cannot be answered directly from the text.

★

1. What are five different fields of business?
2. What are some specializations within the field of finance?
3. What are some different types of managerial careers?
4. What field of business is shown in the box on the far right of Figure 1?

5. What are some specializations within this field?

6. In the box that is second from the left, what information is presented?

7. What kinds of questions should you ask in order to choose a suitable and successful career?

★★ 8. The reading states, "Business is an increasingly important activity throughout the world today." *Does this general statement apply to your own country? *Why or why not? *What opportunities are there for business careers in your country?

9. *Can you add any more business fields or careers to Figure 1? If you do not know the names in English, describe the work.

★ B. Circle the letter of the answer that best completes each of the sentences below.

1. The opportunities for a business career have:
   a. not grown in variety or number
   b. grown in variety and number
   c. grown in number but not variety
   d. grown in variety but not number

2. A person working in computers and data processing may specialize in:
   a. computer programming
   b. computer operating
   c. systems analyzing
   d. all of the above

3. A bookkeeper is a specialist within the field of:
   a. accounting
   b. data processing
   c. finance
   d. marketing

4. In choosing a business career, one might ask questions regarding:
   a. one's area of interest
   b. one's aptitude
   c. job opportunities
   d. all of the above

Vocabulary Exercises

★★ A. Substitute appropriate terms for the italicized words or phrases in the sentences below.

careers	field	aptitude	✔ advancement	consequently
variety	offer	suitable	specialize in	salary

1. Because computers and data processing is a growing field, the opportunities for *upward movement* are great. _____advancement_____

2. There is a wide *range* of careers in the business world. _____

3. The employee quit his job because of the poor *amount of money earned*. _____

4. The *area* of marketing offers different types of jobs, such as advertiser or distributor. _____

5. The computer programmer had a(n) *appropriate* job because he didn't like to work with people. _____

6. Business *professions* offer opportunities in the areas of management, marketing, accounting, finance, and computers and data processing. _____

7. Because the young accountant had a(n) *special capability* for mathematics, he was very successful. _____

8. A person may *train in* different types of management, such as personnel or production management. _____

★★★ **B. Discuss the following questions with a partner. In giving your answers, try to use the italicized terms.**

1. What are the five *fields* of business? Which of these *fields* interests you the most? Within that *field*, which *specialization* do you find the most interesting?

2. Do you know what the *demand* is for this specialization in your country? What do you know about *salary* and opportunities for *advancement*?

3. What questions should one ask before choosing a *career*? Do you think answers to these questions guarantee a *suitable* choice? Why or why not?

4. What skills do you think a bookkeeper should have an *aptitude* for? What skills should a manager have an *aptitude* for? What skills do you have an *aptitude* for?

5. Some of the factors people consider when choosing jobs are listed below. Discuss each factor with your partner. Add to the list as you think of other factors. Then work alone to rank the factors according to their importance to you in choosing a job. Write the most important factor at the top of your list and the least important at the bottom. When you have finished, compare the results with your partner and other members of the class.

personal satisfaction _____ most

opportunities for *advancement* _____ ↑

salary _____

good hours, vacations, etc. _____

geographical location _____

type of work performed _____

variety of tasks _____

_____ _____

_____ _____

_____ _____ ↓

_____ _____ least

★★ C. Fill in the blanks below with the most appropriate terms from the list.

| various | demand | offer | specialize in | salary |
| career | aptitude | advancement | suitable | ✔ field |

Within the _____*field*_____ of accounting, there are a number of areas that you might _____. These include bookkeeping and the _____ types of accounting. In order to choose the specific accounting job that is most _____, you might ask yourself how much this type of work interests you and if you have any _____ for organizing financial data. You might also consider the average _____ earned by a bookkeeper or accountant and the current _____ for the work, particularly for the area in which you hope to live. Opportunity for _____ in the accounting field is another factor that you, as a prospective bookkeeper or accountant, may wish to consider.

Text Analysis

★★ Look at the reading to answer these questions.

1. What does each of the following refer to?

LINES	WORDS	REFERENTS
9	each of these fields	_____
18	these kinds of questions	_____

2. In the reading, two transition phrases are used to give examples. What are these two phrases? What examples do they introduce?

TRANSITION PHRASES   EXAMPLES

_____ → _____

_____ → _____

3. A transition word is used in the reading to show a result. What is this transition? What is the result?

_____ → _____
(transition)   (result)

4. Writers sometimes ask questions in order to focus and intensify the reader's interest. When the reader comes to one of these questions, he or she generally pauses and considers the question before going on. An answer is not expected. This type of question is known as a "rhetorical question."

Find three rhetorical questions in the reading and write them below.

a. _____

_____

b. _____

_____

c. _____

_____

5. Write definitions for the following business fields by matching a field on the left with a definition on the right. Use this definition form:

term being defined → verb *to be* → definition

a. Management

- the handling of large amounts of information generated by business operations

b. Marketing

- the measurement and communication of financial information

c. Accounting

- the acquisition and utilization of capital in order to start up, operate, and expand a company

d. Finance

✔ • the series of activities guiding a company to accomplish its objectives

e. Data Processing

- the movement of goods and services from manufacturer to customer in order to satisfy the customer and to achieve the company's objectives

a. *Management is the series of activities guiding a company to accomplish its objectives.*

_____

b. _____

_____

c. _____

_____

d. _____

_____

e. _____

_____

Classification

⭐ A. Information is frequently classified by arranging it in a chart. Figure 1 on page 12 is a chart that shows the classification of business fields. There are five members of this class. Refer to this chart for the information to complete the following classification of business fields.

Class: Business Fields

Members: *Management*

_____

_____

_____

Management, marketing, accounting, finance, and computers and data process ing may also be considered as separate classes with members of their own. Fill in the blanks below, based on the information provided in Figure 1 on page 12.

Class: _____   Class: Management Careers

Members: _____ Researcher _____   Members: _____

_____   _____

_____   _____

_____   _____

_____

Class: _____

Members: _____

_____

_____ Stockbroker _____

_____

_____

★★★ **B.** In each of the examples below, three of the items are members of the same class and one is not. Cross out the one that is *not* a member. Then write the name of the class to which the other three belong.

CLASS

1. buyer/~~banker~~/seller/distributor   *marketing careers*

2. banker/financial analyst/stockbroker/accountant   _____

3. computers and data processing/finance/
   marketing/general manager   _____

4. computer operator/computer programmer/
   data processing/systems analyst   _____

5. general manager/management/
   production manager/personnel manager   _____

6. advertising/management/marketing/accounting   _____

7. private accountant/banker/government
   accountant/bookkeeper   _____

Information Transfer

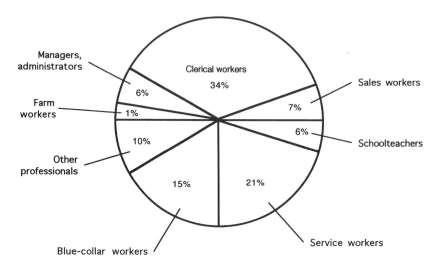

Where Women Are Employed in the U.S.*

Managers, administrators — 6%

Farm workers — 1%

Other professionals — 10%

Clerical workers 34%

Sales workers — 7%

Schoolteachers — 6%

Blue-collar workers — 15%

Service workers — 21%

*Reprinted by permission of The Conference Board from *The Working Woman: A Progress Report*, New York, 1984.

Figure 2

★ **A. Scan Figure 2 to answer these questions.**

1. For each pair of words, circle one word that applies to this graph.
   a. men/women
   b. employed/unemployed
   c. all the world/U.S.
   d. percentage/total number
   e. bar graph/pie graph

2. Using the words you circled, write a sentence to summarize the information provided in this graph.

   _____

   _____

3. What percentage of women are employed as schoolteachers? _____

   What percentage are employed as blue-collar workers? _____

4. Which kind of work employs 21% of women? _____

   7%? _____

5. Which area employs the largest percentage of women? _____

   Which area employs the smallest? _____

6. How many categories of work does this graph include? _____

18   *Part I*

★★★   **B. Refer to Figure 2 to answer these questions.**

1. What are some specific jobs that might be included within the category "other professionals"? _____

     _____

     What are some specific jobs that might be included within the category "clerical workers"? _____

2. What are "blue-collar workers"? _____

     _____

3. Do the numbers in this graph add up to 100? _____ What information does this graph provide about women in the U.S. who are not employed? _____

     _____

4. How does this U.S. employment pattern for women compare to the employment of women in your country? _____

     _____

5. Do you think the pattern (in either the U.S. or your country) will change in the next 20 years? _____ If yes, how will it change and why?

     _____

     Do you think these changes will be positive or negative? _____
     Why? _____

     _____

Additional Activities

1. Skim the want ads of the local newspaper. Note which kinds of business jobs need to be filled. Telephone and inquire about one that interests you. Find out about responsibilities, training or educational requirements, salary, vacations, insurance, benefits, etc.
2. Skim a college catalog to see what business programs are offered. Note the majors, courses, and degrees available.
3. Interview (and tape-record) native and nonnative speakers of English about their career choices. Share one of your interviews with the rest of the class.

Business Basics 1.3: CHOOSING A CAREER

Warm-Up

1. Look at the career path in marketing. In choosing a job it is important to consider what your career path for that occupation could be.

Approx. Years of Service[1]

Years	Position
15—	Vice president marketing
14— 13— 12—	National sales or advertising manager
11— 10—	Product group manager
9— 8—	Marketing staff analyst
7— 6—	Regional sales manager
5— 4—	Branch sales manager
3— 2—	Sales supervisor
1—	Sales

[1]These estimates only approximate yearly progress in a purely hypothetical organization. More specific information is nearly impossible to obtain due to the wide variances between employers.

Reproduced from *Business: Its Nature and Environment, an Introduction,* by Richard Steade, James Lowry, and Raymond Gloss, with the permission of South-Western Publishing Co., Copyright 1984 by South-Western Publishing Co. All rights reserved.

Figure 3

2. What does career *path* mean? _____

   Which position is the entry-level job? _____

   What is the most senior position? _____

   Approximately how many years does it take to become a product group manager?

3. Are you familiar with career paths for other occupations? If you are, draw one on a separate sheet of paper (or on an overhead transparency) and share it with the class.

Preparation

1. In choosing a career or when changing jobs, it is important to analyze your personal strengths and weaknesses. Look at the characteristics listed in the survey below and discuss the meanings of these characteristics as needed.

   Analyze your own strengths and weaknesses by writing a number between one and five beside each characteristic:

   5 = very strong
   4 = somewhat strong
   3 = neither strong nor weak
   2 = somewhat weak
   1 = very weak

SURVEY: STRENGTHS AND WEAKNESSES   1-5

1. ability to get along well with others   _____

2. cooperativeness   _____

3. creativity   _____

4. intelligence   _____

5. academic background (grades/marks and degrees)   _____

6. leadership ability   _____

7. oral communication skills   _____

8. written communication skills   _____

9. technical skills   _____

10. work experience   _____

Now discuss your personal survey with a close friend or relative and get his or her opinion. If necessary, modify your answers based on his or her input.

2. Learning about yourself is essential for career planning. Deciding what is really important to you will help you make difficult career decisions more easily. The following questions are designed to help you learn about yourself.

   Answer the following questions. Discuss your responses and compare them with other people's responses in the class.

CAREER QUESTIONS	ANSWERS
1. Is geographic location important to you?	
2. Do you prefer to lead or follow?	
3. Do you work better alone, in a small group, or in a large group?	
4. Do you work more effectively under pressure or with a minimum of stress?	
5. Do you like to try new ways of doing things or do you prefer established routines?	
6. Do you communicate well orally?	
7. Do you communicate well in writing?	
8. Are you a good listener?	
9. What characteristic do you like best in people you work with?	
10. What kind of job do you want to have in five years?	
11. _____	
12. _____	

Think of other career questions, add them to the questionnaire, and write your answers. How do the answers to these questions help someone in choosing a career?

Integrated Task

1. Working in small groups, read and discuss the following business case.*

SPORTCO LTD.: A CAREER CHOICE

J. M. Sun is the senior product marketing manager for a highly successful line of athletic wear known worldwide by its trademarked logo. He has just received a phone call from the division's vice president, who is his boss. After the usual pleasantries and discussion of some "hot" issues, the vice president invites him to lunch the next day.

Earlier a fax had been passed to Mr. Sun concerning a new vacancy in a key overseas regional office. This position is for a regional marketing manager, and it is an important step to moving upward within Sportco Ltd.'s marketing division.

Mr. Sun has a difficult decision to make. The new job overseas would mean a 20 percent pay increase, plus a very generous overseas living allowance. However, the regional marketing manager position requires a three-year commitment.

Mr. Sun has a number of concerns. First, he is afraid of being so far away from the corporate headquarters and does not want to lose his connection with the successful athletic product line. Second, he is worried about the impact on his family—his wife, 9-year-old son, and 12-year-old daughter. Finally, he is not sure what the next career step would be after the overseas assignment. Yet after 16 years with Sportco Ltd. and 4 years in his current position, he is looking for new challenges.

*For more information about the case study method, see Appendix C. For additional cases, see Appendix D.

2. Mr. Sun, who is your co-worker, comes to you for advice. If the vice president offers him the overseas position, what should Mr. Sun say? In small groups discuss what you would advise and why.

Follow-Up

1. Interview two people regarding their career paths. After you interview them, draw career paths similar to the one used for marketing on page 20. Include both the positions each person has held and the number of years spent in each job. In small groups, compare and discuss these career paths.
2. Do a ten-year projection of your own career path. Include projected positions, years in each position, and salary. Use the marketing career path as a model.
3. In small groups, compare the results of either "Survey Strengths and Weaknesses" or "Career Questions" on pages 21 and 22. Analyze the responses. Then summarize the differences and similarities among the members of your group in an oral presentation.
4. Visit an employment or career planning office. Find out as much as you can about a particular career that interests you and write a report. You could also consult the career section of business textbooks. For example, *Business Today*, fourth edition, by David Rachman and Michael Mescon (New York: Random House, 1985), contains an appendix that lists careers in management, marketing, finance, computers, and data processing (pages 576-585).

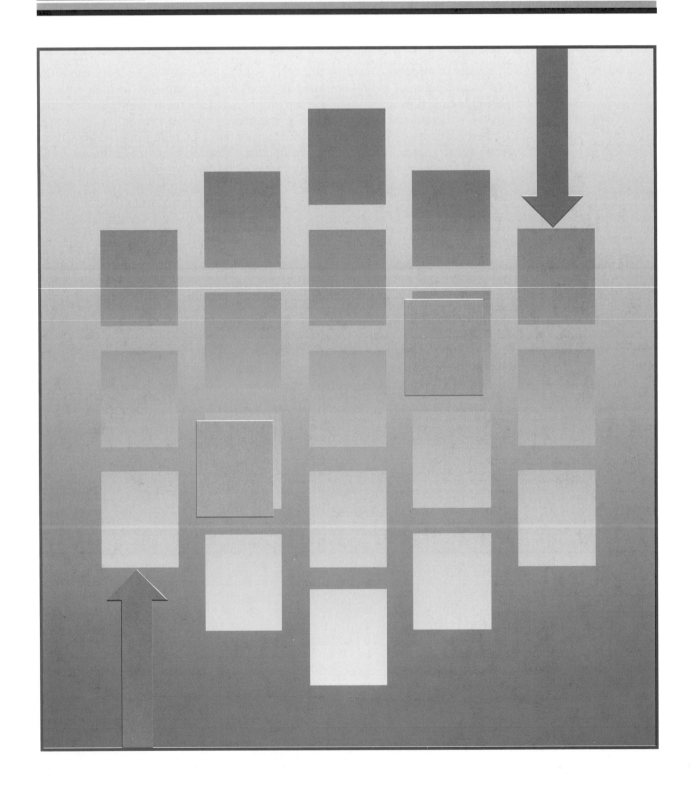

The Global Marketplace

2. Marketing

2.1 The Four P's

2.2 The Target Market

2.3 Market Research and Product Design

3. International Business

3.1 Why Nations Trade

3.2 Multinational Corporations

3.3 Exploring Foreign Markets: Customs and Cultures

2. *Marketing*

Marketing 2.1: THE FOUR P'S

Prereading Activity

Discuss the following questions.

1. What do you think of when you see the term *marketing*? Write down your ideas.
   buyer, competition, advertising

2. Can you list the various steps or actions that are involved in the marketing process? (Think of all the steps that must take place to get goods and services to the customer.)

3. Now write a definition of marketing using some of the ideas and steps listed in Questions 1 and 2.

Marketing is _____

_____

_____

Compare your definition with the ones written by your classmates. Add to your definition if you find any new information.

Vocabulary

Below is a list of terms that you will find in the text. As you read "The Four P's," see if you understand each term. Use this as a working list and add other terms that you do not know.

NOUNS	VERBS	ADJECTIVES	OTHERS
marketing	satisfy	complex	popularly
objective	achieve	vital	_____
element	insure	personal	_____
the four P's	charge	_____	_____
option	price	_____	
competitor	take place		
price leader	_____	_____	
channel of	_____		
distribution	_____		
wholesaler			
retailer			
promotion			
_____			
_____			
_____			

Reading

THE FOUR P'S

Buying, selling, market research, transportation, storage, advertising—these are all part of the complex area of business known as marketing. In simple terms, marketing means the movement of goods and services from manufacturer to customer in order to satisfy the customer and to achieve the company's objectives.

5   Marketing can be divided into four main elements that are popularly known as the four P's:[1]

- product
- price
- placement
10   • promotion

Each one plays a vital role in the success or failure of the marketing operation.

The product element of marketing refers to the good or service that a company wants to sell. This often involves research and development (R & D) of a new product, research of the potential market, testing of the product to insure

15   quality, and then introduction to the market.

A company next considers the price to charge for its product. There are three pricing options the company may take: *above*, *with* or *below* the prices that its competitors are charging. For example, if the average price of a pair of women's leather shoes is $47, a company that charges $43 has priced *below* the market; a

20   company that charges $47 has priced *with* the market; and a company that charges $53 has priced *above* the market. Most companies price *with* the market, selling their goods or services for average prices established by major producers in the industry. The producers who establish these prices are known as price leaders.

The third element of the marketing process—placement—involves getting

25   the product to the customer. This takes place through the channels of distribution. A common channel of distribution is:

manufacturer ➔ wholesaler ➔ retailer ➔ customer

Wholesalers generally sell large quantities of a product to retailers, and retailers usually sell smaller quantities to customers.

30   Finally, communication about the product takes place between buyer and seller. This communication between buyer and seller is known as promotion. There are two major ways promotion occurs: through personal selling, as in a department store; and through advertising, as in a newspaper or magazine.

The four elements of marketing—product, price, placement, and promotion

35   —work together to develop a successful marketing operation that satisfies customers and achieves the company's objectives.

[1]E. Jerome McCarthy, *Basic Marketing* (Homewood, Ill.: Richard D. Irwin, Inc., 1971), pp. 44–46.

Comprehension

A. Answer the following questions about marketing. Questions with asterisks (*) cannot be answered directly from the text.

★

1. What is marketing?
2. *How does the definition of marketing that is given in the reading differ from the one that you wrote?
3. What are the four main elements of marketing?
4. What is involved in the product element of marketing?
5. What are the three pricing options that a company may take?
6. *Using $275 as an average price for word processing software, what are examples of pricing *above*, *with*, and *below* the market?

★★

7. What does placement involve?
8. *Do you think McDonald's provides food on a wholesale or retail basis?
9. *What are some advertising media besides magazines and newspapers?
10. *If you were to specialize in one of the marketing elements, which one would you choose—product, price, placement, or promotion? *Why?

★ B. Circle the letter of the answer that best completes each of the sentences below.

1. The four main elements of marketing are popularly known as:
   a. the movement of goods and services
   b. the four P's
   c. the four M's
   d. buying, selling, market research, and storage

2. The product element refers to:
   a. the four P's
   b. testing of a product to insure quality
   c. the good or service that a company wants to sell
   d. getting the product to the customer

3. Most companies price:
   a. *with* the market
   b. *below* the market
   c. *beyond* the market
   d. *above* the market

4. A common channel of distribution is:
   a. wholesaler → retailer → manufacturer → customer
   b. manufacturer → retailer → wholesaler → customer
   c. retailer → manufacturer → wholesaler → customer
   d. manufacturer → wholesaler → retailer → customer

5. The two major forms of promotion are:
   a. radio and television
   b. personal selling and advertising
   c. personal selling and newspapers
   d. selling advertisements

Vocabulary Exercises

★★ **A.** Write down any terms that you did not understand in the reading. Find each term in the reading, look at its context, and try to figure out the meaning. Discuss these terms with your classmates.

★★ **B.** Look at the terms in the left-hand column and find the correct synonyms or definitions in the right-hand column. Copy the corresponding letters in the blanks.

1. __e__ insure (line 14)	a. choice
2. _____ retailer (line 28)	b. set as a price
3. _____ price *with* the market (line 21)	c. one who sells in small amounts to customers
4. _____ option (line 17)	d. please
5. _____ competitor (lines 17–18)	✔ e. guarantee
6. _____ personal (line 32)	f. the path goods take when moving from manufacturer to customer
7. _____ objective (line 36)	g. private; relating to an individual
8. _____ satisfy (line 35)	h. accomplish
9. _____ take place (line 30)	i. charge an average price
10. _____ channel of distribution (line 26)	j. occur; happen
11. _____ charge (line 18)	k. rival; opponent
12. _____ achieve (line 36)	l. goal

★★ **C.** Fill in the blanks with the most appropriate terms from the list.

vital	insure	retailer	prices	placement
wholesaler	price leader	take place	charge	✔ channel of distribution

The most common _channel of distribution_ is manufacturer → wholesaler → _____ → consumer. Distribution can, however, _____ through slightly modified channels. For example, products are sometimes sold directly by the _____ or the manufacturer, rather than by the retailer. Generally, wholesalers _____ lower _____ than retailers and sell in larger quantities. Together, these channels of distribution play a _____ role in the _____ element of marketing.

Text Analysis

Look at the reading to answer these questions.

1. What does each of the following refer to?

LINES	WORDS	REFERENTS
1	these	_____
11	each one	_____
13	R & D	_____
25	this	_____

2. The reading discusses the four elements of the marketing operation. What are these four parts?

   a. *product* _____

   b. _____

   c. _____

   d. _____

3. What connective words or phrases, if any, are used to introduce each marketing element? If no connective is used, indicate this with Ø.

CONNECTIVES	MARKETING ELEMENTS
a. _____	_____
b. _____	_____
c. *The third element*	*placement*
d. _____	_____

4. a. In line 6, what does the number [1] mean?

   _____

   b. What is the information at the bottom of the page called?

   _____

   c. Why is reference made to *Basic Marketing?*

   _____

5. Sometimes the definition of a term takes this form:

   The production, distribution, ➔ is ➔ known as ➔ business
   and sale of goods and services
   for a profit

   definition ➔ verb *to be* ➔ known as ➔ term being
                                                  defined

Two terms are defined this way in the reading. Find and copy these definitions in the spaces below.

a. *The producers who establish these prices are* _____

_____

b. _____

_____

6. Change the definitions so that the term being defined comes first.

Business ➔ is ➔ the production, distribution, and sale of goods and services for a profit

term being defined ➔ verb *to be* ➔ definition

a. *Price leaders are* _____

_____

b. _____

_____

Classification

★★ Various problems that might occur in the marketing process are listed below. Determine which of the four P's each problem is most closely related to. Mark the appropriate category of *product, price, placement,* or *promotion* with an X.

	PRODUCT	PRICE	PLACEMENT	PROMOTION
1. The advertising gives false information.				x
2. The product is dangerous.				
3. The product is not available in enough stores.				
4. The product is too expensive.				
5. A salesclerk is rude.				
6. The product is sold during the wrong season.				
7. The product is of poor quality.				
8. The advertising is offensive.				
9. The price of a product increases faster than the rate of inflation.				
10. The product is not available in your favorite stores.				

Think of other problems. Then discuss whether they are related to product, price, placement, or promotion.

Writing

1. Read the following letter of complaint about a dangerous product. It is written to be sent as a fax (facsimile transmission).

FACSIMILE TRANSMISSION

TO: Product Safety Manager
LOCATION: L & R Toy Company
FAX TEL: (302) 326-4610
                    STM   DEM
FROM: Susan T. and Donald E. Murphy
LOCATION: 2473 N.E. 15th Street, Portland, Oregon 97201
FAX TEL: (503) 745-2389

DATE: November 14, 1993

Dear Product Safety Manager:

   In September of this year we purchased a toy truck (product #17348) from a retail outlet in Portland. Our son, who is four years old, was playing with the truck about two weeks later when he severely cut his hand on a sharp edge inside the right door of the truck.

   When we returned the truck to the store, the manager refunded our money and apologized for what happened to our son. He said that he would report the accident to the manufacturer, L & R Toy company. However, he said he would continue to sell the toy trucks in his store unless he was notified to return them to L & R Toy Company.

   We feel that L & R Toy Company must immediately recall product #17348 from the market and stop selling this toy until it is safe for children to play with. No other children should be hurt by the sharp edges in the way our son was.

   We await your prompt reply and resolution of this safety problem.

---

2. With a partner, refer to the Classification exercise on page 32. Choose one situation to complain about. Discuss the specifics of the problem with a partner; for example, if the product is of poor quality, exactly what is wrong?

3. With your partner, write a response to Susan and Donald Murphy or write your own letter of complaint. Send it as a fax or letter.

Additional Activities

1. Look at the sale advertisements for grocery stores in the local newspaper. Decide which store has the most competitive prices.

2. Interview the manager of a supermarket and ask from whom the following products are purchased: apples, canned peaches, and fresh chickens. Ask about other products that interest you.

3. Write a letter of complaint about a product that does not satisfy you. Get the address of the manufacturer from the package.

Marketing 2.2: THE TARGET MARKET

Prereading Activity

Discuss the following questions.

1. In a successful marketing operation, do the four elements of product, price, placement, and promotion work together or in isolation? Give a reason to support your answer.

2. If you were a market researcher, what questions would you ask before introducing a product to the market? These examples are given in the reading: "Who is going to buy the product?; "What is the potential to sell this product?" Think of other questions that might be asked using *what, where, when* and *why*.

Why will a customer want to buy the product?

_____

_____

_____

_____

_____

Vocabulary

Below is a list of terms that you will find in the text. As you read "The Target Market," see if you understand each term. Use this as a working list and add other terms that you do not know.

NOUNS	VERBS	ADJECTIVES	OTHERS
strategy	determine	potential	in order to
isolation	focus on	correct	
combination	direct	_____	_____
marketing mix	appeal to		_____
target market	attempt	_____	_____
market	match		
research	mold	_____	
habit	depend on		
identification	blend		
	reach		
_____			
_____	_____		
_____	_____		
	_____		

Reading

THE TARGET MARKET

The marketing strategies of determining product, price, placement, and promotion are not planned in isolation. Marketing analysts often look at a combination of these four factors. This combination of the four P's is known as the marketing mix. The elements of the marketing mix focus on the consumer. In order to develop a successful marketing mix, researchers first ask two important questions:

- Who is going to buy the product?
- What is the potential to sell this product?

The group of customers or consumers who will probably buy the product is known as the target market. The company directs its marketing efforts toward this group of potential customers who form the target market. Once market researchers have determined the target market they wish to appeal to, the company can develop an appropriate mix of product, price, placement, and promotion. The company attempts to match consumer needs or mold consumer desires to the product being offered. For example, if the target market is middle-class teenagers, the marketing mix might consist of the following:

Product:	blue jeans
Price:	*with* the market
Placement:	department store
Promotion:	advertisements on a "pop music" radio station

A successful marketing mix depends on the knowledge about consumers and their buying habits, gained through market research as well as correct identification of the target market. Strategies of product, price, placement, and promotion are blended in order to reach a chosen group of consumers.

Comprehension

A. Answer the following questions about the target market. Questions with asterisks (*) cannot be answered directly from the text.

★

1. What is the marketing mix?
2. What do the elements of the marketing mix focus on?
3. What is the group of customers who will probably buy the product known as?
4. *Why are the consumers who make up the target market for a product referred to as "potential" customers?
5. What does a successful marketing mix depend on?
6. Complete the diagram below with the elements of the marketing mix:

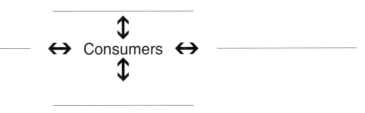

Figure 1

★★   7. *Why are the arrows in the figure two-way rather than just one-way?

8. *Why are consumers at the center of the diagram?

9. Consider the example of middle-class teenagers as the target market for blue jeans. *In what places besides department stores could the product be sold? *What other types of promotion could be used?

10. *If the target market for blue jeans were factory workers, how would the marketing mix change?

★★   B. **Determine which of the following statements are *true* and which are *false*. Then put *T* or *F* in the blanks. Rewrite false statements to make them true.**

1. __*T*__ Knowledge about consumer buying habits is essential in developing a successful marketing mix.

2. _____ The company focuses on production in its marketing strategy.

3. _____ Product and promotion combine to form the complete marketing mix.

4. _____ The company directs its marketing efforts toward the target market.

5. _____ The marketing strategies of product, price, placement, and promotion are planned separately.

Vocabulary Exercises

★   A. **Substitute appropriate terms for the italicized words or phrases in the sentences below.**

attempt	habits	isolation	reaches	matches
✔ potential	focus on	in order to	depends on	strategies

1. Market researchers determine *possible* customers for a product—those consumers whom they think will buy it. _____*potential*_____

2. A successful company *relies on* good promotion to communicate with customers. _____

3. Today television *comes into the homes of* millions of people every day. _____

4. The elements of the marketing mix *concentrate on* the consumer. _____

5. Companies *try* to meet the needs and desires of the individuals who ultimately buy and use their products. _____

6. A successful marketing operation *puts together* the product with customer needs or desires. _____

7. Marketing *plans of action* are developed after thorough research into each of the four P's. _____

8. A company engages in market research *to* develop the most appropriate marketing mix. _____

★ **B. Complete the sentences with the noun and verb forms provided.**

1. **identification/identify**

   a. Market researchers ____identify____ the target market for a particular product.

   b. When an employee joins a large company, he or she is given an

   _____ card.

2. **promotion/promoted**

   a. Advertising agencies are concerned with the _____ of a product.

   b. Last week the boss _____ John because of his outstanding

   work in the accounting department.

3. **competitor/compete**

   a. In the marketplace, businesses _____ with each other.

   b. Sony is a major _____ of General Electric.

4. **determination/determines**

   a. The combination of the four P's _____ the marketing mix.

   b. An accountant makes an accurate _____ of the expenses of a

   company.

5. **isolation/isolated**

   a. Strategies of product, price, placement, and promotion are not planned in

   _____ .

   b. The company doctor _____ the sick employee in the room at

   the end of the hall.

★★ **C. Discuss the following questions with a partner. In giving your answers, try to use the italicized terms.**

1. Which type of promotion *appeals to* you the most—radio, television, magazine, or newspaper advertising?
2. How are the buying *habits* of consumers influenced by promotion?
3. What do you think the *target market* would be for a Rolls-Royce? For microwave ovens? For tennis shoes?
4. What are some of the factors that the market price of a product *depends on*?

Text Analysis

Look at the reading to answer these questions.

★ 1. What does each of the following refer to?

LINES	WORDS	REFERENTS
3	this combination	_____
11	this group	_____
12	they	_____
3,4	factors, elements	_____

★★ 2. In the reading, one connective phrase is used to give an example. What example does it introduce?

_____   →   _____
         (connective)   (example)

3. Find two rhetorical questions in the reading and write them below.

a. _____

_____

b. _____

_____

4. In the reading, two terms are defined using this form:

definition → verb *to be* → known as → term being defined

Find and copy these definitions in the spaces below.

a. *This combination of the four P's is* _____

_____

b. _____

_____

5. Now change the order of the definitions so that the term being defined comes first.

term being defined → verb *to be* → definition

a. *The marketing mix is* _____

_____

_____

b. _____

_____

_____

Application

★★★   A. In the following exercise, determine the marketing mix that you think would be successful for this particular group of consumers (target market). First, look back at the example in the reading. Then fill in the price, placement, and promotion you think would be most effective for the target market that is listed.

     1. Target market: upper-income, middle-aged adults

       Product: Rolls-Royce

       Price: _____

       Placement: _____

       Promotion: _____

     2. Target market: small restaurants

       Product: microwave ovens

       Price: _____

       Placement: _____

       Promotion: _____

     3. Target market: teenagers

       Product: tennis shoes

       Price: _____

       Placement: _____

       Promotion: _____

★★★   B. Choose a target market (for example, elementary school children) and develop the four P's in a marketing mix that you think will reach your chosen group of consumers.

       Target market: _____

       Product: _____

       Price: _____

       Placement: _____

       Promotion: _____

Present your marketing mix to the class. Give reasons to support the product, price, placement, and promotion elements you have chosen.

Information Transfer

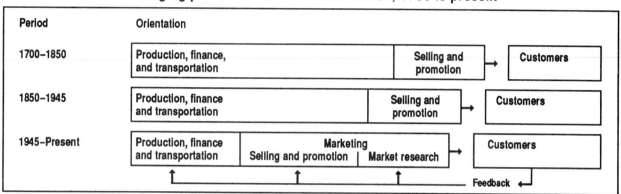

Changing patterns of business orientation, 1700 to present*

*Figure from *Business: An Introduction* by Benjamin M. Compaine and Robert F. Litro, copyright © 1984 by The Dryden Press, reproduced by permission of the publisher.

Figure 2

★★ A. Scan Figure 2 to answer these questions.

1. What category of business orientation is the largest in the period 1700–1850? _____ From 1850 to 1945? _____

2. In which time period do customers have the greatest representation? _____

3. Which time period has the greatest variety of orientations? _____ What are they? _____

4. Which two time periods have basically the same orientations? _____

5. Which period of time is the longest? _____ Which is the shortest? _____

★★★ B. Refer to Figure 2 to answer these questions.

1. Why do you think the first time period ends in 1850? _____

   Why does the second time period end in 1945? _____

2. In which direction do the arrows point in the periods 1700–1850 and 1850–1945? _____

In which direction do the arrows point for the period 1945–present?

_____

Why is this feedback loop important? _____

_____

3. How does the position of selling and promotion change from the 1850–1945 period to the present? _____

_____

4. Why has market research been included in the third time period? _____

_____

5. In general, how have the patterns of business orientation changed? _____

_____

What are some reasons for these changes? Consider such factors as economics, technology, and politics. _____

6. What do you predict the pattern of business orientation will look like from 2000 to 2050? Draw a diagram to represent this.

Additional Activities

1. Bring in an advertisement and analyze it with regard to its intended target market. Decide what type of appeal is being made (to the senses, to economy, etc.). Also analyze the advertisement for its factual representations and its implications. Compare your observations with those of your classmates.
2. Walk around a city or town and write down five advertisements. Discuss and share these ads with the class.
3. Interview a representative from a local company about his or her company's marketing mix and target market.
4. Develop a questionnaire and interview someone about his or her favorite kind of automobile. Try to determine why this particular car has more appeal than the others.

Marketing 2.3: MARKET RESEARCH AND PRODUCT DESIGN

Warm-up

1. Look at the bottle of shampoo below and draw lines to match the words with the parts of the bottle.

Name of manufacturer

Slogan

Name of product

Container

Label

Cap (or lid)

2. Read the information on the label and fill in the blanks below.

Name of shampoo _____

Manufacturer (company) _____

Size (in ounces) _____ Price _____

Slogan _____

3. Who do you think the target market is for this shampoo? Does this shampoo appeal to you? Why or why not?

Preparation

1. Discuss where people can buy shampoo. Name as many local stores as possible where shampoo is sold.
2. With a partner, visit one of the stores mentioned above. Complete the following survey based on what you see in the store.

MARKET RESEARCH SURVEY*

Name of store _____ **Address** _____

Brand of shampoo	**Price/oz.**	**Color**	**Slogan**
1.			
2.			
3.			
4.			
5.			

Total number of different brands of shampoo _____

Description of containers or packages (Draw several designs below.)

Target market for each of the five brands of shampoo listed above

1. _____

2. _____

3. _____

4. _____

5. _____

Description of the shampoo that appeals to you most

_____

_____

Reasons you like it

_____

_____

_____

---

*Note: You may use another product instead of shampoo, for example, soft drinks or calculators. If you choose a different product, then revise the Market Research Survey as needed.

Integrated Task*

1. Working in small groups, discuss the results of your market research.
2. Design your own shampoo or other product. Include the following information.

   Name of product _____

   Price/ounce _____ Size (in ounces) _____

   Shape of container _____

   Color of container _____ Color of product _____

   Slogan _____

   On another piece of paper, draw the container and label for your product. Include the name, price, number of ounces, and slogan.

3. Determine the marketing mix that you think will be successful for your product. Be as specific as possible.

   Target market: _____

   Product: _____

   Price: _____

   Placement: _____

   Promotion: _____

*Note: If you use a product other than shampoo, revise this exercise to include what is necessary in designing this product.

Follow-up

1. Draw your group's product for the rest of the class (on the blackboard or an overhead transparency). Choose someone from your group to present your product to the rest of the class. This person should explain your marketing mix and why your product will be successful.
2. With a partner, write a one-minute radio commercial for your product. Practice your commercial and then read it to other members of the class.
3. In small groups, create a commercial about your product for television. Include any necessary props. Videotape your commercial or present it "live" to the class.
4. Design and conduct a market research survey to find out consumer preferences for a particular product, such as shampoo. Compile your results and write a summary.

3. *International Business*

International Business 3.1: WHY NATIONS TRADE

Prereading Activity

Discuss the following questions.

1. What are some advantages of international trade? Consider this from the perspectives of both importer *and* exporter.

   Importer—can get greater variety of products,

   _____

   _____

   _____

2. What are some disadvantages of international trade? Again, consider both parties.

Exporter—becomes too dependent on foreign markets,

_____

_____

_____

3. What commodities does your country export? What are the three biggest imports?

_____

_____

_____

Vocabulary

Below is a list of terms that you will find in the text. As you read "Why Nations Trade," see if you understand each term. Use this as a working list and add other terms that you do not know.

NOUNS	VERBS	ADJECTIVES	OTHERS
resource	restrict	national	efficiently
output	import	global	domestically
standard of living	lack	scarce	
expertise	export	advantageous	_____
absolute advantage	suit		_____
comparative advantage	enable	_____	_____
	_____	_____	
_____	_____	_____	
_____	_____		
_____			

Reading

WHY NATIONS TRADE

The sale of goods and services is not restricted to local, regional, or national markets; it often takes place on an international basis. Nations import goods that they lack or cannot produce as efficiently as other nations, and they export goods that they can produce more efficiently. This exchange of goods and ser-
5 vices in the world, or global, market is known as international trade. There are three main benefits to be gained from this type of exchange.

First, international trade makes scarce goods available to nations that need or desire them. When a nation lacks the resources needed to produce goods domestically, it may import them from another country. For example, Saudi Arabia
10 imports automobiles; the United States, bananas; and Mexico, computers.

Second, international trade allows a nation to specialize in production of those goods for which it is particularly suited. This often results in increased output, decreased costs, and a higher national standard of living. Natural, human, and technical resources help determine which products a nation will specialize
15 in. Saudi Arabia is able to specialize in petroleum because it has the necessary natural resource; Mexico is able to specialize in the production of wooden furniture because it has the human resources to assemble the furniture by hand; and the United States is able to specialize in the computer industry because it has the technical expertise necessary for design and production.

20 There are two economic principles that help explain how and when specialization is advantageous. According to the theory of absolute advantage, a nation ought to specialize in the goods that it can produce more cheaply than its competitors or in the goods that no other nation is able to produce. According to the theory of comparative advantage, a nation ought to concentrate on the products
25 that it can produce most efficiently and profitably. For example, a nation might produce both grain and wine cheaply, but it specializes in the one that will be more profitable.

The third benefit of international trade is its political effects. Nations that trade together develop common interests that may help them overcome political
30 differences. Economic cooperation has been the foundation for many political alliances, such as the European Community (EC), founded in 1957.

International trade has done much to improve global conditions. It enables countries to import goods they lack or cannot produce domestically. It allows countries to specialize in certain goods with increased production and decreased
35 prices. Finally, it opens the channels of communication among nations.

Comprehension

A. Answer the following questions about international trade. Questions with asterisks (*) cannot be answered directly from the text.

★   1. What are the various markets in which the sale of goods and services takes place?
    2. What is international trade?
    3. What is the first benefit of international trade?

4. What is one commodity that Mexico imports? *Why?
5. What resources help determine which products a nation will specialize in?
6. *Which of these resources is most abundant in your country?
★★ 7. According to the theory of comparative advantage, what should a nation do?
8. *Can you give an example to show how this theory has worked in your country? Explain.
9. What is the third benefit of international trade?
10. *What are some examples, other than the European Community, of how economic cooperation has helped overcome political differences?

★ B. Circle the letter of the answer that best completes each of the following sentences.

1. Nations import goods they:
   a. produce efficiently
   b. specialize in
   c. lack or cannot produce efficiently
   d. do not need or desire

2. Specialization often results in:
   a. increased output
   b. decreased costs
   c. higher standard of living
   d. all of the above

3. The United States is able to specialize in the computer industry because of its
   _____ resources.
   a. natural
   b. technical
   c. human
   d. international

4. According to the theory of comparative advantage, a nation should concentrate on the product that:
   a. it can specialize in
   b. no other nation can produce
   c. it can make efficiently
   d. it can produce most efficiently and profitably

5. The European Community is based on:
   a. cooperation
   b. one company
   c. competition
   d. political differences

Vocabulary Exercises

★★ A. Substitute appropriate terms for the italicized words or phrases in the following sentences.

global	domestic	suit	expertise	resource
output	enables	lack	efficiently	✔ scarce

1. Diamonds are found in only a few places in the world; they are rare. _____*scarce*_____

2. The *production* of the factory increased when ten new workers were hired.

   _____

3. Nations that *are without* technological resources cannot produce their own computer systems. _____

4. International trade has affected *worldwide* conditions in numerous ways.

   _____

5. *Specialized knowledge* is necessary to design fax machines. _____

6. Many small businesses focus only on the *home* market. _____

7. Oil is a valuable *asset*. _____

8. International trade *makes it possible* for countries to import goods that they cannot produce. _____

★★ **B. Complete the sentences with the noun, verb, and adjective forms provided.**

1. **restriction/is restricted/restrictive**

   a. A _____*restriction*_____ limits the number of workers that can be hired.

   b. Trade _____*is*_____ not _____*restricted*_____ to national markets.

   c. A _____*restrictive*_____ trade law is one that controls the number of goods imported or exported.

2. **specialization/specializes/specialized**

   a. Generally a nation that _____ in certain products can increase output.

   b. Research and development is a _____ area of marketing.

   c. America's _____ in agriculture has made it a leading producer of grain.

3. **importation/imports/imported**

   a. The United States _____ coffee.

   b. _____ goods are sometimes subject to a special tax.

   c. The continued U.S. dependence on the _____ of oil is a controversial issue.

4. **production/produces/productive**

   a. The _____ of steel is an important industry in a developed economy.

   b. Managers try to motivate employees to be efficient and _____ .

   c. France _____ excellent wines.

50   *Part II*

5. **suitability/is suited/suitable**

   a. Because California has a warm climate, oranges are a _____ product for it to specialize in.

   b. The _____ of a particular specialization is determined by the country's resources.

   c. Because of its cold climate, Sweden _____ not _____ to specialize in coffee or bananas.

★★★   C. **Discuss the following questions with a partner. In giving your answers, try to use the italicized terms.**

   1. What natural *resources* does your country have?
   2. What are some goods your country does not *produce domestically*? Why doesn't it *produce* these goods? (Use *lack* and natural, human, or technical *resources* in your answer.)
   3. Do you think international trade raises the *standard of living*? Has it raised the *standard of living* in your country? If so, how?
   4. Do you have *expertise* in any of the business fields? Are there any other areas in which you have *expertise*, such as in sports, music, or art?
   5. What kinds of *restrictions*, if any, do you think should be placed on international trade?

Text Analysis

★★   **Look at the reading to answer these questions.**

   1. What does each of the following refer to?

LINES	WORDS	REFERENTS
6	this type of exchange	_____
8	them	_____
12	this	_____
26	one	_____

   2. The reading discusses three benefits of international trade. What are these three benefits?

    a. *makes scarce goods available to nations that need or desire them*

    b. _____

    c. _____

   3. What connective words or phrases are used to introduce each benefit?

CONNECTIVES		BENEFITS
a. *first*	→	*makes scarce goods available*
b. _____	→	_____
c. _____	→	_____

4. What are some other connective words or phrases that could have been used instead of *second* and *third*?

a. _____

b. _____

5. The reading discusses the resources that help determine which products a nation will specialize in. The possession of a particular resource may be thought of as a *cause* and the resultant specialization may be seen as an *effect*. List the cause/effect specialization relationships for Saudi Arabia, Mexico, and the United States.

cause
↓
effect

a. *Saudi Arabia has the natural resource petroleum.*

↓

Saudi Arabia has specialized in petroleum.

b. *Mexico* _____

↓

_____

_____

c. _____

↓

_____

_____

Classification

★★★ Some possible results of international trade are listed below. Look at each situation and determine whether it concerns countries that import or export. Then decide whether it is an advantage or a disadvantage for those nations. Enter the number of the situation in the appropriate area of the grid.

✔ 1. A greater variety of goods is available.
2. Foreign competition endangers domestic industries.
3. A larger market is now available.
4. A nation becomes too dependent upon its foreign markets.
5. More jobs are created.
6. Gross National Product (GNP) is increased.
7. A nation becomes too dependent on foreign products.
8. For economic reasons, a country prefers to sell to foreign markets rather than deal with its domestic market.
9. Domestic workers lose employment.
10. A nation imports natural resources rather than depleting its own sources.

11. The international market gets flooded.
12. The national standard of living is raised.

	Importing nations	Exporting nations
Advantage	*1*	
Disadvantage		

Writing

★★ **Write a paragraph describing a product your country has specialized in. Include in your paragraph information about resources, economic theory, and results.**

Example:

One of the products that Japan has chosen to specialize in is production of cameras. Because of its technical resources, Japan has the knowledge required to design and produce sophisticated cameras; because of its human resources, Japan has a work force that is large enough to produce these cameras on a competitive basis. According to the theory of comparative advantage, Japan has chosen to specialize in production of cameras because it can produce them more cheaply than it can a number of other goods. Japan's specialization in cameras has resulted, among other things, in increased domestic employment, more money coming into the country, and a higher standard of living.

Additional Activities

1. Develop a questionnaire and interview local residents about their attitudes toward imported products.
2. View and discuss a videotape entitled "Wilde About Trade," which is part of the World of Economics Curriculum Series, and may be ordered from the Federal Reserve Bank of San Francisco, P.O. Box 7702, San Francisco, CA 94120-9990.
3. Visit the electronics section of a department store. Take an inventory of certain products (e.g., stereos, televisions, or radios) and note which are domestic products and which are imported. Share the results with your classmates.

International Business 3.2: MULTINATIONAL CORPORATIONS

Prereading Activity

Discuss the following questions.

1. The next reading discusses the development of multinational corporations. International Business Machines (IBM), Royal Dutch Shell, Panasonic, Coca-Cola, and Volkswagen are listed as examples of these corporations. List other multinational corporations that you can think of.

2. What multinational businesses are found in your country? Write the names in English or your native language.

_____

_____

_____

_____

3. A multinational corporation is primarily based in one country. Where are the following multinational corporations based?

   a. IBM   *United States*_____

   b. Royal Dutch Shell   _____

   c. Panasonic   _____

   d. Coca-Cola   _____

   e. Volkswagen   _____

Tell where the multinationals that you listed in Questions 1 and 2 are based.

Vocabulary

Below is a list of terms that you will find in the text. As you read "Multinational Corporations," see if you understand each term. Use this as a working list and add other terms that you do not know.

NOUNS	VERBS	ADJECTIVES	OTHERS
corporation	involve in	raw	primarily
relationship	expand	domestic	
development	view		_____
stage	operate in	_____	_____
base	vary		
subsidiary		_____	
appreciation of	_____		
	_____		
_____			
_____			
_____			

Reading

MULTINATIONAL CORPORATIONS

A company often becomes involved in international trade by exchanging goods or services with another country—importing raw materials it may need for production or exporting finished products to a foreign market. Establishing these trade relationships is the first step in the development of a multinational business. At this stage, however, the corporation's emphasis is still on the domestic market. As trade expands, the corporation's dealings with companies or people outside the "home country" of that corporation increase.

The corporation then begins to view the whole world as a base for production and marketing operations. The next step in the development of a multinational business is focusing on the world market. The company may establish a foreign assembly plant, engage in contract manufacturing, or build a foreign manufacturing company or subsidiary. Therefore, a multinational corporation is a company that is primarily based in one country and has production and marketing activities in foreign countries.

Since World War II, multinational corporations have grown rapidly. The names and products of many of the multinationals have become well-known in the world marketplace: International Business Machines (IBM), Royal Dutch Shell, Panasonic, Coca-Cola, and Volkswagen. Coca-Cola, for example, now has operations in more than 180 countries.

A multinational corporation operates in a complex business environment. Cultural, social, economic, political, and technological systems vary from country to country. In order to operate successfully, a multinational company needs a basic understanding and appreciation of the foreign business environment.

Comprehension

A. Answer the following questions about multinationals. Questions with asterisks (*) cannot be answered directly from the text.

1. What is the first step in the development of a multinational business?
2. Where is the company's emphasis when it is simply trading with other countries?
3. What market does a multinational corporation focus on?
4. A company may establish its manufacturing operations in foreign countries. What are three forms that these operations may take?
5. What is a multinational corporation?
6. When have multinationals grown rapidly? *Why do you think they have experienced this period of rapid growth?
7. *What are some products that are produced by the following multinational corporations: IBM, Coca-Cola, Panasonic, Shell, and Volkswagen?
8. *Why does a multinational corporation operate in a more complex business environment than a domestic company?
9. *What are some of the social and political factors that can vary from country to country?
10. Why does a multinational corporation need a basic understanding of foreign business environments? *How can a multinational gain this understanding?

★★ **B.** Determine which of the following statements are *true* and which are *false*. Then put *T* or *F* in the blanks. Rewrite false statements to make them true.

1. __*T*__ Multinational corporations have grown rapidly since 1945.

2. _____ Any company engaged in international trade is a multinational business.

3. _____ In order to operate successfully, a multinational company needs to be aware of national and international business environments.

4. _____ A multinational corporation focuses on its "home country," or domestic market.

5. _____ A multinational company does not establish factories in foreign countries.

Vocabulary Exercises

★★ **A.** Write down any terms that you did not understand in the reading. Find each term in the reading, look at its context, and try to figure out the meaning. Discuss these terms with your classmates.

★ **B.** Look at the terms in the left-hand column and find the correct synonyms or definitions in the right-hand column. Copy the corresponding letters in the blanks.

1. __*j*__ corporation (line 5)   a. chiefly; principally

2. _____ expand (line 6)   b. function in; work in

3. _____ view (line 8)   c. change

4. _____ stage (line 5)   d. a company having more than half of its stock owned by another company

5. _____ primarily (line 13)   e. increase the dimensions of

6. _____ base (line 8)   f. growth; expansion

7. _____ vary (line 21)   g. see; look at

8. _____ subsidiary (line 12)   h. foundation

9. _____ operate in (line 20)   i. a step in development

10. _____ development (line 4)   ✔ j. a type of business organization formed by an association of stockholders

★★★ **C.** Fill in the blanks in the following paragraph with the most appropriate terms from the list.

base	operate in	appreciation of	expands
vary	corporation	✔ development	subsidiary
stages	involved in	view	relationships

During the ___*development*___ of a corporation, the organizational structure may

_____ over time and pass through a number of _____ . As

the _____ grows, it _____ its operations. It might become

_____ setting up a _____ . Although the corporation still has a primary or "home _____ ," establishment of a subsidiary allows the company to enter into new _____ with a _____ toward increasing its production and marketing capabilities.

Text Analysis

Look at the reading to answer these questions.

★   1. What does each of the following refer to?

LINES	WORDS	REFERENTS
2	it	_____
5	this stage	_____
17	IBM	_____

2. Match the connective words or phrases with the appropriate functions.

_____ however (line 5)   a. summarizing

_____ then (line 8)   b. illustrating

_____ therefore (line 12)   c. contrasting

_____ for example (line 18)   d. sequencing information

★★★   3. Summarize the two general steps in the development of a multinational corporation.

a. _____

_____ (lines 3–5)

b. _____

_____ (lines 8–10)

4. Sometimes the definition of a term takes this form:

A restrictive trade law →   is → a law → that → controls the number of goods imported or exported

term being defined → verb *to be* → class → $\begin{Bmatrix} that \\ which \end{Bmatrix}$ → definition

This type of definition is known as a formal definition. In a formal definition the term or word being defined occurs first. It is followed by the verb *to be* (usually *is* or *are*). Next the class states the general group that the term belongs to:

TERMS	CLASSES
multinational corporation	company
typewriter	business machine
absolute advantage	theory of specialization

After the class, either *that* or *which* is used. Finally, the definition itself includes information distinguishing this term from other members of its class.

Write formal definitions for multinational corporation (page 56), corporation (page 57), and subsidiary (page 57).

a. *A multinational corporation is a company that* _____

_____

_____

_____

b. _____

_____

_____

_____

c. _____

_____

_____

_____

5. Formal definitions may be shortened to a more general form, which includes less information. This is often called a semiformal definition. The class, *that* or *which*, and the verb *to be* are omitted.

A restrictive trade law ➔ controls ➔ the number of goods imported or exported

term being defined   ➔ verb   ➔ definition

Change the formal definitions from the previous exercise into semiformal definitions.

a. *A multinational corporation is primarily based* _____

_____

_____

b. _____

_____

_____

_____

c. _____

_____

_____

_____

Application

★★★ The rapid growth of multinational corporations has been criticized in several areas. Some people feel that these corporations have become too powerful and control certain markets. Others argue that multinationals are not subject to the social or political controls of any one country because they have operations in many different countries.

Divide into two groups to discuss multinationals from different perspectives.

Group1: Residents of third-world countries

What are some of the potential dangers in the rapid growth of multinationals?

_____

_____

_____

_____

_____

Group 2: Executives of multinational corporations

What are some of the benefits that nations and individuals might receive because of the existence of multinationals?

_____

_____

_____

_____

_____

Listen to reports from both groups. Then discuss the following question with your classmates:

Considering both the advantages and disadvantages, do you favor increased growth of multinational companies? Why or why not?

_____

_____

_____

_____

_____

Information Transfer

World Exports of Rice (Milled Basis), by Country of Origin   In Thousands of Metric Tons

Country or region	Calendar year					
	1987	1988	1989	1990	1991[1]	1992[2]
United States	2,444	2,247	2,973	2,424	2,200	2,300
Argentina	150	160	130	70	75	60
Australia	338	417	450	470	470	500
Burma	493	368	456	186	300	500
China	1,020	698	320	300	550	500
Taiwan	240	104	68	50	200	100
EC -12	981	920	963	969	1,040	1,160
Egypt	105	108	100	32	125	125
Guyana	69	56	26	30	30	20
India	350	200	450	420	500	400
Indonesia	100	0	104	50	0	0
North Korea	154	199	175	75	0	0
Pakistan	1,226	950	779	904	1,200	1,200
Thailand	4,355	4,791	6,037	3,927	4,200	4,500
Uruguay	190	244	251	250	250	350
Vietnam	153	97	1,400	1,500	1,000	800
Other	560	371	419	387	351	404
World Total	12,928	11,930	15,101	12,044	12,491	12,919

[1] Preliminary   [2] Forecast

Courtesy of Foreign Agricultural Service, U.S.D.A., 1991.

Figure 1

★★   **A. Scan Figure 1 to answer these questions.**

    1. What commodity does this chart provide information about? _____

    2. How many exporters of rice are represented? _____

    3. For which years does this chart provide information? _____

    4. Which year had the highest world total for exportation of rice? _____

       How many metric tons were exported that year? _____

    5. In 1987, which country exported the least amount of rice? _____

       How many metric tons? _____

    6. In which year did Argentina export the most rice? _____

    7. In which year did Taiwan export the least amount of rice? _____

    8. For the year 1988, what does the number 200 refer to? _____

    9. For the year 1992, what does the number 4,500 refer to? _____

★★★ **B. Refer to Figure 1 to answer these questions.**

1. Which country exported the most rice during the period of 1987–1992? _____ Why do you think this country is the world leader in the exportation of rice? _____

_____

2. In 1988, Vietnam *produced* 14,600,000 metric tons of rice. How many metric tons did Vietnam *export* that year? _____ What accounts for the difference between these two figures? _____

3. Look at the world totals for exportation of rice from 1987–1992. Rank the years in order of highest exportation to lowest.

_____ , _____ , _____ , _____ , _____ , _____

What are some conditions that might account for these fluctuations? _____

_____

_____

4. In your opinion, what are some advantages and disadvantages when a country specializes in the production of rice for export?

_____

_____

_____

Additional Activities

1. Find and bring magazine advertisements to class. See if they are for domestic companies or multinationals.
2. List two or three foreign subsidiaries in your country and discuss their products or services.
3. Develop a questionnaire and interview a business professional about the role of multinationals in the world marketplace.

International Business 3.3: EXPLORING FOREIGN MARKETS: CUSTOMS AND CULTURE

Warm-up

1. Look at the following Coca-Cola logos.*

a. _____

b. _____

c. _____

d. _____

e. _____

f. _____

*Coca-Cola and the Dynamic Ribbon device are registered trademarks of The Coca-Cola Company.

Figure 2

2. Match each logo with the country it represents. Write the name of the country below the logo. Compare answers with your partner.
   Russia   Morocco   Mexico   Poland   China   Germany
   Check your answers with the answer key on page 65.
3. Why does The Coca-Cola Company need to use a different logo in each country? Is it important to keep some part of the logo the same? Why or why not?

Preparation

1. Discuss the following cross-cultural questions with a partner from another country. Choose an answer together and circle it. When you are finished, check your answers with the answer key.

   a. Gift giving is very common in Japan. When a Japanese business acquaintance gives you a wrapped gift, what should you do?

      1. Open the gift in front of the person who gave it to you.
      2. Thank the person and open the gift at a later time.
      3. Return the gift and explain that it is not necessary to exchange gifts.

b. You are attending a business meeting in Saudi Arabia. Someone asks you to pass the sugar for his coffee. Which hand do you use?

1. right
2. left
3. either one, depending on whether you are left- or right-handed

c. In business dealings with Koreans, which color should be avoided when writing a Korean person's name?

1. red
2. black
3. blue

d. In general, which of the following topics would be good to avoid during a conversation with Latin American business acquaintances?

1. sports
2. travel
3. local politics

e. In which of the following countries should you *not* tip?

1. Iceland
2. Great Britain
3. the United States

2. Write one question about your country's culture and customs, using the same format as the questions above.

3. Give your question to the teacher. After the teacher has collected all the questions, discuss them. Explain your question and answer to the class.

Integrated Task

1. You have been assigned the role of special advisor to an international business group who will be setting up a business in your country's capital city. These people are not from your country.

If possible, work with a partner from your country or a similar area of the world. Write the name of your country or area of the world on the blank line.

_____

(your country or area of the world)

Your job is to give the business officials advice about the customs and culture of your country so they can operate most effectively in the foreign market. Use the list of considerations below to help you decide on important cultural aspects of your country. Make brief notes regarding aspects you should explain to the multinational business representatives.

Dress
- How to dress (suit, casual clothes, etc.)
- Special colors that should *not* be worn

Formalities
- How to greet the host (bow, shake hands, etc.)
- Whether or not to bring a gift, and what kinds of gifts might be appropriate
- Who should initiate the actual business part of the meeting (the host or the foreign guest)

Time
- Time to arrive at a business meeting
- Days and hours of work

Nonverbal behavior
- How close together people should sit at the meeting
- Whether or not eye contact is acceptable

Sociological concerns
- Attitude toward work in your culture
- How decisions are made
- How women in business are viewed
- The role of bribes, if any

Additional cultural considerations important for business negotiations in your country

- _____
- _____
- _____

2. Using the list of considerations you developed in Exercise 1 above, work with a partner from a different country. Roleplay a business meeting in which you advise your partner about the best way to set up a business in your country. Then switch roles.

Follow-up

1. Choose three or four of the most important things to consider while doing business in your country. Present these to the whole class.
2. As a class, work together to make a list of the cross-cultural differences and similarities you discovered in doing business in various countries. Draw a chart or diagram to summarize your data.
3. Have a panel discussion about the different cultures and customs around the world. Have one representative of each country be a member of the panel. Videotape your discussion.
4. Work with someone from your country or area of the world to design marketing strategies for a new multinational business in your country. Keep in mind the cultural aspects that you have discussed.

Answer key

Coca-Cola Company logos: a. China, b. Mexico, c. Poland, d. Germany, e. Russia, f. Morocco.

Cross-cultural questions: a. 2, b. 1, c. 1, d. 3, e. 1.

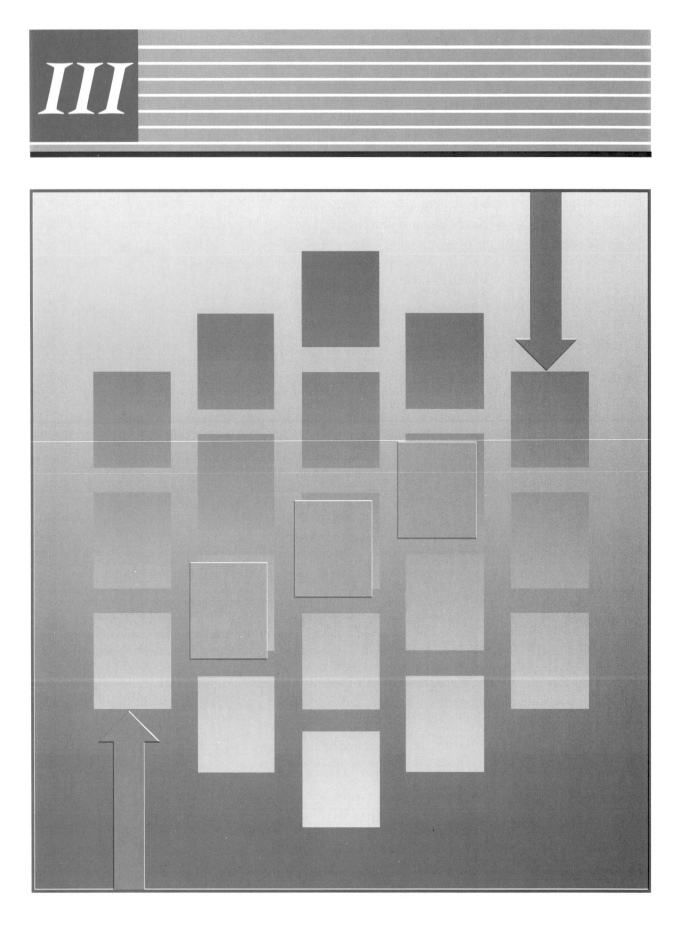

Financial Aspects of Business Operations

4. Accounting

4.1 An Accounting Overview

4.2 The Balance Sheet

4.3 Preparing an Income Statement

5. Finance

5.1 Why Finance?

5.2 Acquisition of Capital

5.3 Acquiring Start-up Capital for a Small Business

4. Accounting

Accounting 4.1: AN ACCOUNTING OVERVIEW

Prereading Activity

Discuss the following questions.

1. What do you think of when you see the term *accounting*? Quickly write down words or ideas as they come into your mind.

figures, record-keeping, bookkeeper,

2. What steps or actions does an accountant take in order to provide accurate financial information about a company?

   collecting financial data,

   _____

   _____

   _____

3. Are there different types of accountants in your country? Explain what kind of work they do and for whom they work.

   _____

   _____

   _____

   _____

Vocabulary

Below is a list of terms that you will find in the text. As you read "An Accounting Overview," see if you understand each term. Use this as a working list and add other terms that you do not know.

NOUNS	VERBS	ADJECTIVES	OTHERS
party	communicate	informed	while
status	interpret	standardized	independently
procedure	monitor	rigorous	solely
financial statement	reflect		whereas
agency	allow	_____	
fee	earn		_____
	fulfill	_____	
_____	hire		_____
	maintain	_____	
_____			_____
	_____		
	_____		
	_____		

Reading

AN ACCOUNTING OVERVIEW

Accounting is frequently called the "language of business" because of its ability to communicate financial information about an organization. Various interested parties, such as managers, potential investors, creditors, and the government, depend on a company's accounting system to help them make

5   informed financial decisions. An effective accounting system, therefore, must include accurate collecting, recording, classifying, summarizing, interpreting, and reporting of information on the financial status of an organization.

In order to achieve a standardized system, the accounting process follows accounting principles and rules. Regardless of the type of business or the

10   amount of money involved, common procedures for handling and presenting financial information are used. Incoming money (revenues) and outgoing money (expenditures) are carefully monitored, and transactions are summarized in financial statements, which reflect the major financial activities of an organization.

15   Two common financial statements are the balance sheet and the income statement. The balance sheet shows the financial position of a company at one point in time, while the income statement shows the financial performance of a company over a period of time. Financial statements allow interested parties to compare one organization to another and/or to compare accounting periods

20   within one organization. For example, an investor may compare the most recent income statements of two corporations in order to find out which one would be a better investment.

People who specialize in the field of accounting are known as accountants. In the United States, accountants are usually classified as public, private, or gov-

25   ernmental. Public accountants work independently and provide accounting services such as auditing and tax computation to companies and individuals. Public accountants may earn the title of CPA (Certified Public Accountant) by fulfilling rigorous requirements. Private accountants work solely for private companies or corporations that hire them to maintain financial records, and governmental

30   accountants work for governmental agencies or bureaus. Both private and governmental accountants are paid on a salary basis, whereas public accountants receive fees for their services.

Through effective application of commonly accepted accounting systems, private, public, and governmental accountants provide accurate and timely

35   financial information that is necessary for organizational decision-making.

Comprehension

A. Answer the following questions about accounting. Questions with asterisks (*) cannot be answered directly from the text.

★
1. Why is accounting called the "language of business"?
2. How is a standardized accounting system achieved?
3. What are revenues and expenditures?

★★   4. What do the balance sheet and the income statement have in common? How are they different?

5. *How might the information contained in financial statements be useful to managers? *How might creditors use this information?

6. How are accountants classified in the United States?

7. What kinds of services do public accountants provide?

8. What is a CPA? *Do you have a similar type of position in your country? *Explain.

9. *Which type of accounting—public, private, or governmental—appeals to you the most? *Why?

10. *What are some management decisions that might be based on accounting information?

★★   **B.** Circle the letter of the answer that best completes each of the sentences below.

1. Accounting information is used by _____ to help them make financial decisions.
   a. managers
   b. potential investors
   c. creditors
   d. all of the above

2. Regardless of the type of business or the amount of money involved:
   a. all companies use identical accounting systems
   b. balance sheets are more important than income statements
   c. common procedures are used in handling financial information
   d. no standardized accounting system is employed

3. Business monetary transactions are summarized in:
   a. bank books
   b. financial statements
   c. computers
   d. cash registers

4. Public accountants may earn the title of CPA by:
   a. becoming governmental accountants
   b. paying a fee
   c. fulfilling rigorous requirements
   d. obtaining a Bachelor of Arts degree in accounting

5. Private and governmental accountants are paid on a _____ basis.
   a. salary
   b. monthly
   c. fee
   d. weekly

Vocabulary Exercises

★★ **A.** Substitute appropriate terms for the italicized words or phrases in the sentences below.

status	agencies	monitored	maintain	independently
procedure	fee	hire	✔ rigorous	solely

1. Many accounting departments have *strict* entrance requirements; only the most qualified applicants are allowed to enter these programs. _rigorous_

2. The particular *method* used to process employee insurance claims may vary from company to company. _____

3. The stock market is *closely watched* every day. _____

4. Rather than expand into foreign lines, the dress shop manager chose to deal *only* with domestic fashion designers. _____

5. Although the consultant's *charge for services* was high, his guidance and advice were well worth the money. _____

6. The financial *condition* of a company is reflected in its financial statements. _____

7. When the business began to expand, a second bookkeeper was brought in to help *keep* the books. _____

8. In the United States there are numerous *organizations that provide services* at the local, state, and national levels. _____

★★ **B.** Complete the sentences with the noun, verb, and adjective forms provided.

1. **communication/to communicate/communicative**
   a. Supervisors should strive for two-way ___*communication*___ with their employees.
   b. By using an overhead projector, the guest speaker was able ___*to communicate*___ his statistical information clearly.
   c. Because of the clerk's highly developed ___*communicative*___ skills, she was given a position that required her to deal directly with customers.

2. **information/informed/informative**
   a. The owner _____ his employees that they would all receive a 5 percent pay increase.
   b. *Getting Acquainted with Accounting*, by John L. Carey, is a very _____ book.
   c. Financial _____ is essential for organizational decision making.

3. **allowance/allowed/allowable**

    a. The supervisor lost control of his staff members after he _____ them to override his decisions.

    b. When the factory was built 50 years ago, little _____ was made for remodeling and expansion.

    c. Although _____, smoking was discouraged in the lunch room.

4. **fulfillment/fulfill/fulfilling**

    a. At times the assembly line worker felt a lack of professional

       _____.

    b. When he was promoted to production supervisor, however, his job became much more _____.

    c. Before the accountant could become a CPA, she had to _____ a number of requirements.

5. **standards/has standardized/standard**

    a. The _____ paper size in the United States for business letters and memoranda is 8½ X 11 inches.

    b. The computer department _____ its procedures for storing and retrieving data.

    c. Nowadays rigorous _____ are enforced in the area of food processing and packaging.

★★★   C. **Fill in the blanks below with the most appropriate terms from the list.**

parties	✔ financial statement	reflected	standardized	allows
whereas	interpretations	informed	communicates	rigorous

    An income statement is one example of a *financial statement*. It _____ financial information about a company over a period of time. A _____ format is used to present the financial information. This _____ interested _____ to compare one income statement to another in order to make _____ financial decisions. But there is still a great deal of risk involved in financial decision making because the information _____ in an income statement is subject to a variety of _____.

Text Analysis

Look at the reading to answer these questions.

★

1. What does each of the following refer to?

LINES	WORDS	REFERENTS
1	its	_____
4	them	_____
19	another	_____
21	one	_____

2. Which connective word in the reading is used to summarize information?

_____

3. Which connective phrase in the reading is used to illustrate a point?

_____

★★

4. Two terms are used to show contrast (lines 17 and 31). Find the terms and copy them below. Then write down the concepts that are being contrasted.

TERMS   CONCEPTS BEING CONTRASTED

a. _____   _____ / _____

b. _____   _____ / _____

5. In lines 24–32, three types of accountants are discussed. What are they? List at least two characteristics for each type of accountant.

TYPES OF ACCOUNTANTS   CHARACTERISTICS

a. *public* _____ → *work independently* _____

_____

b. _____ → _____

_____

c. _____ → _____

_____

6. Read lines 16–20 and then write formal definitions for balance sheet and income statement. Use this form:

term being defined → verb *to be* → class → $\begin{Bmatrix} \text{that} \\ \text{which} \end{Bmatrix}$ → definition

a. *A balance sheet is* _____

_____

_____

b. _____

_____

_____

Writing

★★★ Write a paragraph contrasting the three types of accountants. Begin your paragraph in this way:

Public, private, and governmental accountants differ in several ways.

_____

_____

_____

_____

_____

_____

_____

_____

_____

_____

Additional Activities

1. Ask an accountant to describe his or her job and the duties he or she performs.
2. Interview someone in the accounting department of a large company. Find out what categories are used to monitor incoming and outgoing money.
3. Make a telephone call to a public accountant to see what the fees would be for the following services: a basic business consultation, preparation of a personal income tax return (state and federal), and preparation of a business income tax return (state and federal). Share your results with the class.

Accounting 4.2: THE BALANCE SHEET

Prereading Activity

Discuss the following questions.

1. In order to work with a balance sheet, you need to understand two fundamental terms. Match these two terms with the correct definitions: *assets and liabilities*.

    what a company owes = _____

    what a company owns = _____

2. What are examples of company assets?
    equipment, accounts receivable, _____

    _____

    _____

3. What are examples of company liabilities?

    long-term notes, accounts payable,

    _____

    _____

    _____

4. Have you ever worked with a balance sheet? How did you make use of it?

    _____

    _____

    _____

    _____

Vocabulary

Below is a list of terms that you will find in the text. As you read "The Balance Sheet," see if you understand each term. Use this as a working list and add other terms that you do not know.

NOUNS	VERBS	ADJECTIVES	OTHERS
process	own	particular	internally
condition	owe	receivable	externally
asset	represent	monetary	
property	equal	current	_____
liability	express	payable	
owners' equity	list	long-term	_____
accounting	detail		
equation		_____	_____
inventory			
	_____	_____	
_____			
	_____	_____	
_____			

Reading

THE BALANCE SHEET

Financial statements are the final product of the accounting process. They provide information on the financial condition of a company. The balance sheet, one type of financial statement, provides a summary of what a company owns and what it owes on one particular day.

5   Assets represent everything of value that is owned by a business, such as property, equipment, and accounts receivable. On the other hand, liabilities are the debts that a company owes—for example, to suppliers and banks. If liabilities are subtracted from assets (assets – liabilities), the amount remaining is the owners' share of a business. This is known as owners' or stockholders' equity.

10   One key to understanding the accounting transactions of a business is to understand the relationship of its assets, liabilities, and owners' equity. This is often represented by the fundamental accounting equation: assets equal liabilities plus owners' equity.

ASSETS = LIABILITIES + OWNERS' EQUITY

15   These three factors are expressed in monetary terms and therefore are limited to items that can be given a monetary value. The accounting equation always remains in balance; in other words, one side must equal the other.

The balance sheet expands the accounting equation by providing more information about the assets, liabilities, and owners' equity of a company at a specific

20   time (for example, on December 31, 1993). It is made up of two parts. The first part lists the company assets, and the second part details liabilities and owners' equity. Assets are divided into current and fixed assets. Cash, accounts receivable, and inventories are all current assets. Property, buildings, and equipment make up the fixed assets of a company. The liabilities section of the balance sheet is

25   often divided into current liabilities (such as accounts payable and income taxes payable) and long-term liabilities (such as bonds and long-term notes).

The balance sheet provides a financial picture of a company on a particular date, and for this reason it is useful in two important areas. Internally, the balance sheet provides managers with financial information for company decision-

30   making. Externally, it gives potential investors data for evaluating the company's financial position.

Comprehension

A. **Answer the following questions about the balance sheet. Questions with asterisks (*) cannot be answered directly from the text.**

★   1. What is the final product of the accounting process?

2. What is a balance sheet?

3. Does the balance sheet provide financial information for a long period of time (for example, January to June 1993) or does it provide information for a specific point in time (for example, on June 30, 1993)?

4. What is the difference between assets and liabilities?
5. How is owners' or stockholders' equity determined?
6. How can the relationship between assets, liabilities, and owners' equity be represented?

★★ 7. Does the accounting equation always remain in balance? *Why or why not?
8. How can a business use a balance sheet? *As a manager, how would you find a balance sheet useful?

★★ B. **Complete the balance sheet by writing in the correct terms from the list below.**

✔ assets   current liabilities   long-term liabilities
liabilities   fixed assets   current assets
stockholders' equity

International Manufacturing, Inc.
Balance Sheet
December 31, 1993

Assets				
Cash	$ 49,400		Accounts payable	$ 30,000
Accounts receivable	1,600		Income taxes payable	19,000
Inventories	53,000		Total	$ 49,000
Total	$104,000			
			Bonds	$ 20,000
Property	$ 15,000		Long-term notes	40,000
Buildings	50,000		Total	$ 60,000
Equipment	10,000			
Total	$ 75,000		Total liabilities	$109,000
Total assets	$179,000		Common stock	$ 47,000
			Retained earnings	23,000
			Total	$ 70,000
			Total liabilities and stockholder's equity	$179,000

Figure 1

Vocabulary Exercises

★★   A. Write down any terms that you did not understand in the reading. Find each term in the reading, look at its context, and try to figure out the meaning. Discuss these terms with your classmates.

★   B. Look at the terms in the left-hand column and find the correct synonyms or definitions in the right-hand column. Copy the corresponding letters in the blanks.

1. __g__ property (line 6)

2. _____ equal (line 12)

3. _____ condition (line 2)

4. _____ detail (line 21)

5. _____ accounting equation (line 12)

6. _____ monetary (line 15)

7. _____ process (line 1)

8. _____ express (line 15)

a. assets equal liabilities plus owners' equity

b. provide information item by item

c. indicate by words or symbols

d. have the same value as

e. a series of transactions, changes, or functions that bring about a particular result

f. the existing circumstance

✔ g. anything owned by a person

h. of or pertaining to money

★★★   C. Discuss the following questions with a partner. In giving your answers, try to use the italicized terms.

1. What is the difference between accounts *receivable* and accounts *payable*?
2. Why are accounts *receivable* and cash considered current *assets* while *property* and equipment are considered fixed *assets*? What do you think the difference is between current and fixed *assets*?
3. The *owners' equity* in a company equals *assets* minus *liabilities*. What is meant by *owners'* (or stockholders') *equity*?
4. If you were a manager, how would you use the balance sheet to evaluate your company's financial *condition*?
5. What do you consider your personal *assets*? Do you have any *liabilities*? What are they?

Text Analysis

Look at the reading to answer these questions.

★   1. What does each of the following refer to?

LINES	WORDS	REFERENTS
1	they	_____
9	this	_____
11	this	_____
15	these three factors	_____

★★ 2. In line 6, what are *property, equipment, and accounts receivable* examples of?

_____

3. In line 7, what do *suppliers and banks* refer to?

_____

4. In lines 5–7, two different phrases are used to incorporate examples in the reading. What are these phrases?

a. _____

b. _____

5. Another method of clarification by example is the use of mathematical representations. From the reading, copy examples that use mathematical symbols.

a. _____

b. _____

6. In lines 28–31, two uses of the balance sheet are given. What are the key words that show each of these uses is in a different area? What use does each word introduce?

KEY WORDS   USES

a. _____ → _____

b. _____ → _____

Classification

★★ Categories of the balance sheet can be classified to show the relationship between them. Fill in the following blanks based on the information provided in the reading and in Figure 1 (page 79).

Class: Assets   Class: Liabilities
Members: *Current assets*   Members: _____
          _____   _____

Class: Current assets   Class: _____
Members: _____   Members: Accounts payable
          _____   _____

Class: _____   Class: Long-term liabilities
Members: _____   Members: _____
                                                     _____

          Equipment

Application

★★★ Using the information in the reading, answer the following questions. Give reasons to support your answers.

1. Which of the following is *not* a fixed asset: office equipment, machinery, marketable securities, land, and buildings? Why?

   _____

   _____

2. Are the following liabilities current or long-term: bank loans payable, accounts payable, mortgage bonds payable, taxes payable, and long-term notes payable? List each under the correct heading.

   CURRENT LIABILITIES   LONG-TERM LIABILITIES

   _____   _____

   _____   _____

   _____   _____

3. If a company's assets are $140,017 and its liabilities total $74,215, what is the owners' (or stockholders') equity? Explain how you arrived at this answer.

   _____

   _____

4. The fundamental accounting equation for Burns Manufacturing Company is:

$$\text{Assets} \quad = \text{Liabilities} + \text{Owners' Equity}$$
$$\$40,000 \quad = \quad \$0 \quad + \quad \$40,000$$

   In the business's next transaction, the owner borrows $8,000 from the local bank in the form of a loan. Which of the following statements accurately describes how this transaction affects the accounting equation?

   _____ a. Assets would increase by $8,000 and owners' equity would decrease by $8,000.

   _____ b. Both assets and liabilities would decrease by $8,000.

   _____ c. Assets would increase by $8,000 and liabilities would increase by $8,000.

   _____ d. Liabilities would increase by $4,000 and owners' equity would increase by $4,000.

5. Equity is the amount of money that remains when liabilities are subtracted from assets (assets minus liabilities). Why is a distinction made between owners' equity and stockholders' equity?

   _____

   _____

   _____

Information Transfer

Miles Laboratories, Inc.
Balance Sheet
Year Ended December 31, 19__

Assets		Liabilities	
Current assets		Current liabilities	
Cash	$ 8,814,000	Bank loans	$ 38,242,000
Accounts receivable	$ 59,711,000	Accounts payable	$ 39,745,000
Inventories	$ 68,597,000	Taxes on income	$ 5,613,000
Other	$ 11,901,000	Current portion of	
Total current assets	$149,023,000	long-term debt	$ 21,423,000
		Total current liabilities	$105,023,000
Investments	$ 14,173,000		
Fixed assets		Long-term debt	$ 85,864,000
Buildings	$ 81,920,000	Deferred income tax	$ 6,587,000
Machinery and equipment	$ 85,882,000	Other	$ 573,000
Less depreciation	$ 70,025,000	Shareholder's equity	
Land	$ 7,474,000	Preferred stock, none	
Construction in progress	$ 9,871,000	issued	
Total fixed assets	$115,122,000	Common stock	$ 10,721,000
Other assets		Capital in excess of	
Goodwill and trademarks	$ 53,910,000	par value of stock	$ 39,640,000
Patents and processes	$ 1,515,000	Retained earnings	$ 87,777,000
Other	$ 1,021,000	Less cost of common	
Total assets	$334,764,000	stock held in treasury	[$ 1,421,000]
		Total shareholder's	
		equity	$136,717,000
		Total liabilities and	
		shareholder's equity	$334,764,000

From table on page 420 in *The World of American Business: an Introduction* by Rona B. Cherry and Lawrence B. Cherry. Copyright © 1977 by Rona B. Cherry and Lawrence B. Cherry. Reprinted by permission of Harper & Row Publishers, Inc.

Figure 2

★★ **A. Scan Figure 2 to answer these questions.**

1. What is the long-term debt for Miles Laboratories, Inc.? _____

2. How much are the total current assets of this company? _____
   The total fixed assets? _____ The total assets? _____

3. Which current liability equals $5,613,000? _____

4. Which type of asset is the highest current asset? _____

_____

★★★   **B. Refer to Figure 2 to answer these questions.**

1. There is no total given for long-term liabilities in this balance sheet. Which three categories should be added together to get this total?

   _____

   What are the total long-term liabilities?

   _____

2. What is the accounting equation for Miles Laboratories, Inc., on December 31? (Assets = Liabilities + Owners' Equity)

   _____ = _____ + _____

3. If Miles Laboratories, Inc., sells $50,000 in stock in order to raise capital for a new warehouse, which figures in the balance sheet must be changed?

   _____

   _____

4. Which one of the items listed under shareholders' equity must be subtracted from the total shareholders' equity rather than added to it?

   _____

   _____

Additional Activities

1. Bring in an example of a balance sheet from a company. Compare it with the ones brought in by your classmates.
2. Discuss and compare the balance sheet and the income statement using examples from Merrill, Lynch, Inc., *How to Read a Financial Report* (New York: Merrill, Lynch, Inc.) 1991, or other sources.
3. Call or write to request a copy of a company's annual report.

Accounting 4.3: PREPARING AN INCOME STATEMENT

Warm-Up

1. Look at the following two financial statements.

Thompson Electrical Products, Inc.
Balance Sheet
December 31, 1993

Assets

Cash	$ 32,400
Accounts receivable	31,200
Inventory	38,400
Land	76,800
Building	120,000
Total assets	$ 298,800

Liabilities and Owner's Equity

Liabilities:

Accounts payable	$ 43,200
Mortgage payable	86,400
Total liabilities	$ 129,600

Owners' equity:

Capital stock .... $ 127,200	
Retained earnings 42,000	
Total owners' equity	$ 169,200
Total liabilities and owners' equity	$ 298,800

Thompson Electrical Products, Inc.
Income Statement
For the Month Ended Dec. 31, 1993

Revenues:

Sales revenues	$ 110,400
Less cost of goods sold	[67,200]
Total revenues	$ 43,200

Expenses:

Advertising .... $	2,400
Rent	2,880
Interest .... $	840
Salary .... $	12,000
Other expenses	1,560
Total expenses	$ 19,680
Net income	$ 23,520

Figure 3

2. Review the definitions of a balance sheet and income statement on page 70. Then discuss some of the differences between the two types of financial statements with a partner. How can each type of financial statement be used in business planning?
3. Look at the balance sheet. What are its two basic categories of information?
4. Now look at the income statement. What are its three basic categories? Summarize the kind of information an income statement provides.

Preparation

1. The following list of transactions is for Canterbury Mall. Determine whether each transaction is a revenue or an expense. Mark the appropriate category of revenue or expense with an X.

TRANSACTION		REVENUE	EXPENSE
Rent received from building owned $140,300		_____	_____
Building upkeep (cleaning and repair) 30,000		_____	_____
2% commission on all sales in the building......330,400		_____	_____
Property taxes on the building............................15,700		_____	_____
Insurance on the building..................................10,500		_____	_____
Heating...22,600		_____	_____
Electricity 35,500		_____	_____
Installation of new restroom..............................27,500		_____	_____

2. With a partner, prepare an income statement for Canterbury Mall for the year ended May 30, 1993. Use the transactions from above for your revenue and expenditure entries. The blank form below can be used to help you write up the income statement.

Canterbury Mall
Income Statement
For the Year Ended _____

Revenues:

_____ $ _____
_____ $ _____

Total Revenues $ _____

Expenses:

_____ $ _____
_____ _____
_____ _____
_____ _____
_____ _____
_____ _____

Total expenses $ _____

Net Income $ _____

Figure 4

Integrated Task

1. Working in small groups, read and discuss the following business case.

FINANCIAL DECISIONS IN THE TILE BUSINESS

Humberto Cardenas worked for a number of years as a tile installer for a large and successful tile store. He earned approximately $50,000 per year. When he lost his job due to a recession, he decided to form his own tile company, a small corporation, and become an independent contractor. The following is a summary of the transactions of the business during the first three months of operations in 1993:

Transactions:

Jan.	19	Stockholders invested $21,000 in the business
Feb.	21	Received payment of $4,300 for tiling a bathroom and kitchen
Mar.	5	Paid $140 for an advertisement in the local newspaper
Apr.	10	Received $6,500 for installing tile in two model homes
	13	Paid gas and transportation expenses for truck, $900
	15	Miscellaneous business expenses were paid, $520
	19	Paid dividends to stockholders of $4,700

2. Working in small groups, prepare an income statement in order to decide how Humberto is doing in his new business. (Use the income statement in the Warm-Up as a model.) After preparing the income statement, analyze it and answer the following questions:

   • Should he continue to work as an independent contractor?
   • What are some other considerations (in addition to finances) he should think about in deciding the future of his tile business?

Follow-Up

1. Write your income statement on the blackboard or an overhead transparency. Choose someone from your group to present your income statement and recommendation(s) to the rest of the class. You can use the results of the discussion from Integrated Task Question 2 to help you.
2. You are a financial consultant. Write a brief report explaining what Humberto Cardenas should do regarding his tile business. Be sure to provide support for your recommendation(s).
3. Prepare a financial statement for a one-month period of the revenues and expenditures of someone living in your country.
4. Find annual reports from two or more different companies. Read and compare the financial statements. Decide which of the companies you would prefer as a stock investment.

5. Finance

Finance 5.1: WHY FINANCE?

Prereading Activity

Discuss the following questions.

1. What are some of the primary considerations for an owner starting up a business?

2. How does a company use its money or capital?

3. An individual as well as a company needs to borrow money. When an individual borrows money, it is known as personal financing. Personal financing can be obtained through a short-term or long-term arrangement. What are some examples of short-term and long-term individual financing?

short-term financing: *charge accounts*
_____
_____
_____
_____

long-term financing: *mortgage on a house*
_____
_____
_____
_____

Vocabulary

Below is a list of terms that you will find in the text. As you read "Why Finance?," see if you understand each term. Use this as a working list and add other terms that you do not know.

NOUNS	VERBS	ADJECTIVES	OTHERS
consideration	purchase	primary	similarly
funds	utilize	external	
capital	start up	short-term	
investment	support		
finance	acquire		
credit extension	last		
charge account	obtain		
arrangement	expect		
	repay		

Reading

WHY FINANCE?

One of the primary considerations when going into business is money. Without sufficient funds a company cannot begin operations. The money needed to start and continue operating a business is known as capital. A new business needs capital not only for ongoing expenses but also for purchasing necessary

5   assets. These assets—inventories, equipment, buildings, and property—represent an investment of capital in the new business.

How this new company obtains and uses money will, in large measure, determine its success. The process of managing this acquired capital is known as financial management. In general, finance is securing and utilizing capital to

10   start up, operate, and expand a company.

To start up or begin business, a company needs funds to purchase essential assets, support research and development, and buy materials for production. Capital is also needed for salaries, credit extension to customers, advertising, insurance, and many other day-to-day operations. In addition, financing is

15   essential for growth and expansion of a company. Because of competition in the market, capital needs to be invested in developing new product lines and production techniques and in acquiring assets for future expansion.

In financing business operations and expansion, a business uses both short-term and long-term capital. A company, much like an individual, utilizes short-

20   term capital to pay for items that last a relatively short period of time. An individual uses credit cards or charge accounts for items such as clothing or food, while a company seeks short-term financing for salaries and office expenses. On the other hand, an individual uses long-term capital such as a bank loan to pay for a home or car—goods that will last a long time. Similarly, a company seeks

25   long-term financing to pay for new assets that are expected to last many years.

When a company obtains capital from external sources, the financing can be either on a short-term or a long-term arrangement. Generally, short-term financing must be repaid in less than one year, while long-term financing can be repaid over a longer period of time.

30   Finance involves the securing of funds for all phases of business operations. In obtaining and using this capital, the decisions made by managers affect the overall financial success of a company.

Comprehension

A. Answer the following questions about finance. Questions with asterisks (*) cannot be answered directly from the text.

★

    1. What does a company need in order to begin operations?
    2. What is capital? *Where can capital be acquired?

3. Why does a new business need capital? *What are some examples of ongoing expenses that a company encounters?

★★ 4. What is finance?

5. Why does a company use both short-term and long-term capital?

6. How might a business utilize the short-term capital that it has borrowed?

7. What is the repayment period for short-term financing? For long-term financing?

8. *Have you ever financed anything on a short-term or long-term arrangement? *Explain.

9. *What are some items for which a company might seek short-term financing? *Long-term financing?

★★ B. Determine which of the following statements are *true* and which are *false.* Then put *T* or *F* in the blanks. Rewrite false statements to make them true.

1. __*T*__ Long-term financing is used by a company to purchase new equipment and to construct additional facilities.

2. _____ A new business only needs capital to meet day-to-day expenses.

3. _____ In financing business operations, a company relies almost entirely on short-term financing.

4. _____ Long-term and short-term financing may be acquired from outside sources.

5. _____ How well a company manages its finances affects the overall success of the business venture.

Vocabulary Exercises

★★ A. Substitute appropriate terms for the italicized words or phrases in the sentences below.

acquire	utilizes	primary	arrangement	last
external	consideration	repaid	expect	✔ capital

1. Although Ms. Robinson and her partners had already defined their new product line, they were still searching for the *money* needed to purchase equipment and materials. ___*capital*___

2. In general, a business that is able to manage its finances successfully will *continue to exist.* _____

3. One of the *chief* elements in financial planning is achieving the correct balance between long-term and short-term capital. _____

4. A company needs sufficient funds to *obtain* necessary assets, such as property, buildings, and inventories. _____

5. When a company wants to expand, one *factor* that always affects this decision is cost. _____

6. In making investments, a financial manger *uses* a wide variety of information provided by all departments of the company. _____

7. When an individual or a company borrows money from a bank, this money must be *paid back* by a specific date. _____

8. Owners *anticipate* that the company will use fixed assets for many years.

_____

★★ **B.** **Discuss the following questions with a partner. In giving your answers, try to use the italicized terms.**

1. Do you have any *charge accounts*? Which stores or companies do you have *charge accounts* with?
2. Personal *investments* include savings accounts, real estate, stocks, and precious metals, such as gold. Do you have any personal *investments*? Which kind are they?
3. When most people *purchase* a house, do they pay cash or do they negotiate some type of *financial arrangement*? When they *purchase* a car, do they pay cash or negotiate a *financial arrangement*?
4. If you were to *start up* a small appliance manufacturing company, what fixed assets would you *purchase*?
5. What are some of the *external* sources through which a company *obtains short-term* and long-term *capital*?

★★★ **C.** **Fill in the blanks with the most appropriate terms from the list.**

| similarly | capital | primary | short-term | support |
| consideration | purchase | ✔ start up | arrangements | finance |

The Cunhas were planning to _____*start up*_____ a small retail business. Before making the final decision, they looked at the amount of personal _____ they had to invest. The remaining funds they would have to _____ through various _____ and long-term _____.

Another _____ was the type of equipment they would have to _____ initially. _____, the Cunhas evaluated the costs of inventory, employee salaries and benefits, and other general expenses. After reviewing all these factors, the Cunhas decided to open their business.

Text Analysis

Look at the reading to answer these questions.

★ 1. What does each of the following refer to?

LINES	WORDS	REFERENTS
5	these assets	_____
8	its	_____
31	this capital	_____

★★ 2. In lines 22–23, a connective phrase is used to show contrast. Find the connective phrase and copy it below. Then write down the concepts that are being contrasted.

_____   _____ / _____
     (connective)   (concepts being contrasted)

3. What are each of the following examples of?

LINES	WORDS	EXAMPLES
5	inventories, equipment, buildings, and property	_____
21	clothing and food	_____
23	bank loan	_____

4. What does a new business need capital for?

a. _____ (line 4)

b. _____ (line 5)

5. Two terms are defined in the reading using this form:

definition ➜ verb *to be* ➜ known as ➜ term being defined

Find and copy these definitions in the spaces below.

a. *The money needed to start up and continue operating a business is* _____

_____

_____

b. _____

_____

_____

6. One term is defined using this form:

term being defined ➜ verb *to be* ➜ definition

Find and copy this definition in the space below.

_____

_____

_____

Classification

★★★ Classify the following real-life situations. First decide whether they are examples of short- or long-term financing. Then classify them according to the specific uses of the funds.

SHORT-TERM USES OF FUNDS
(CURRENT ASSETS)

- inventories
- accounts receivable
- cash
- marketable securities

LONG-TERM USES OF FUNDS
(FIXED ASSETS)

- equipment
- buildings
- property

1. To deal with the complexities of inventory control, an electrical wholesale business purchases a minicomputer.

     _____*long-term*_____ / _____*equipment*_____

2. In order to locate its manufacturing site close to the natural resource required for production, a timber company constructs a new plywood mill.

     _____ / _____

3. An American toy manufacturer increases production during the summer months in anticipation of pre-Christmas purchases in the fall.

     _____ / _____

4. Anticipating the need for more employee and customer parking, a local department store purchases a vacant lot adjacent to its store.

     _____ / _____

5. Foreseeing the need to implement a second shift on a production line, an auto manufacturer carries an unusually large balance in the corporate payroll bank account.

     _____ / _____

6. Because a local book wholesaler suddenly receives an influx of early payments from its customers, the business purchases 90-day certificates of deposit through its bank.

     _____ / _____

7. A construction company yielded a higher-than-expected return in a recent project, and with these funds it acquires a future industrial park site.

     _____ / _____

8. To promote a new product in its initial phases of marketing (the first six months), a small appliance manufacturer offers special terms to retailers to introduce this product line.

     _____ / _____

9. In order to maximize the shipping efficiency of a container, a farm equipment manufacturer retains a number of smaller orders until a large shipment can be made.

     _____ / _____

10. A real estate investment firm assists in the loan application process of an insurance company that is building a new downtown office complex.

     _____ / _____

Writing

★★★   Write a letter to a bank or savings-and-loan institution inquiring about the types of short- and long-term financing available. Write the letter either as an individual seeking financial information or as the representative of a company needing additional capital.

Example:

FACSIMILE TRANSMISSION

TO: Anna Alvarez, Manager
LOCATION: Business Finance Dept., National City Bank
           205 Commercial Street, Portland, OR 97203
FAX TEL: (503) 929-4837

FROM: James Smith, President
LOCATION: West Coast Industries
           721 Market Street, San Francisco, CA 94109
FAX TEL: (415) 338-5948

DATE: November 14, 1993

Dear Anna:

As we discussed last week at lunch, West Coast Industries (WCI) plans a major expansion of its cold-storage warehouse operations based in Portland. In order to expand these facilities, WCI will need a combination of short- and long-term financing. Our estimates indicate a need for $1,500,000 for one year and $15,750,000 for a term of ten years. The long-term financing will, of course, be utilized for the construction of the new cold-storage warehouse. Short-term financing will permit the purchase of additional inventory.

Would National City Bank be able to provide WCI with a line of credit totaling $17,250,000 for the purposes of this expansion project? Our executive committee would welcome the opportunity to discuss this proposal in detail with the bank's board of directors at the earliest possible date. Your assistance in arranging a meeting would be most appreciated.

Additional Activities

1. Call or visit a bank and find out what financing options are available to you as an individual.
2. Ask a representative from a bank, savings-and-loan institution, or credit union to describe the various types of financing handled by that particular institution.
3. Collect brochures from a variety of lending institutions. Compare the short- and long-term loans that each offers.

Finance 5.2: ACQUISITION OF CAPITAL

Prereading Activity

Discuss the following questions.

1. This reading discusses the ways financial support may be obtained by a corporation. What is a corporation? Write your own definition of corporation in the space provided below. Begin your definition in this way:

   A corporation is a form of business that

   Compare your definition with the one written by the person next to you. Add to your definition if you find any new information. Then compare your definition with the one given in "International Business" (page 57).

2. A corporation obtains financial support through two different types of financing. Based on your understanding of "equity" and "debt," match these two terms with the correct definitions: *equity financing* and *debt financing*.

    acquisition of borrowed funds = _____

    acquisition of owner funds   = _____

3. One way for a corporation to raise capital is by selling stock. Do you think the purchase of stock is a wise financial investment? Why or why not? Have you ever purchased stock? Describe your experience.

_____

_____

_____

_____

Vocabulary

Below is a list of terms that you will find in the text. As you read "Acquisition of Capital," see if you understand each term. Use this as a working list and add other terms that you do not know.

NOUNS	VERBS	ADJECTIVES	OTHERS
source	borrow	initial	quarterly
stock	exemplify	proportional	
share	entitle	severe	_____
valuation	issue	periodic	
bond	turn to		_____
deadline	meet	_____	
interest payment	force		_____
obligation		_____	
	_____		
_____	_____		
_____	_____		
_____			

Reading

ACQUISITION OF CAPITAL

A corporation needs capital in order to start up, operate, and expand its business. The process of acquiring this capital is known as financing. A corporation uses two basic types of financing: equity financing and debt financing. Equity financing refers to funds that are invested by owners of the corporation.

5   Debt financing, on the other hand, refers to funds that are borrowed from sources outside the corporation.

Equity financing (obtaining owner funds) can be exemplified by the sale of corporate stock. In this type of transaction, the corporation sells units of ownership known as shares of stock. Each share entitles the purchaser to a certain

10   amount of ownership. For example, if someone buys 100 shares of stock from Ford Motor Company, that person has purchased 100 shares worth of Ford's resources, materials, plants, production, and profits. The person who purchases shares of stock is known as a stockholder or shareholder.

All corporations, regardless of their size, receive their starting capital from

15   issuing and selling shares of stock. The initial sales involve some risk on the part of the buyers because the corporation has no record of performance. If the corporation is successful, the stockholder may profit through increased valuation of the shares of stock, as well as by receiving dividends. Dividends are proportional amounts of profit usually paid quarterly to stockholders. However, if the corpo-

20   ration is not successful, the stockholder may take a severe loss on the initial stock investment.

Often equity financing does not provide the corporation with enough capital and it must turn to debt financing, or borrowing funds. One example of debt financing is the sale of corporate bonds. In this type of agreement, the corpora-

25   tion borrows money from an investor in return for a bond. The bond has a maturity date, a deadline when the corporation must repay all of the money it has borrowed. The corporation must also make periodic interest payments to the bondholder during the time the money is borrowed. If these obligations are not met, the corporation can be forced to sell its assets in order to make payments to

30   the bondholders.

All businesses need financial support. Equity financing (as in the sale of stock) and debt financing (as in the sale of bonds) provide important means by which a corporation may obtain its capital.

Comprehension

A. **Answer the following questions about acquisition of funds. Questions with asterisks (*) cannot be answered directly from the text.**

★

     1. Why does a corporation need capital?
     2. What are the two basic types of financing used by a corporation?
     3. From whom are funds acquired for each type of financing?

4. What does one share of stock entitle the purchaser to?
★★ 5. Why do the initial sales of stock involve some risk?
6. How might a stockholder benefit from his or her stocks?
7. If the corporation is not successful, how might the stockholder be affected?
8. How does the corporation benefit from selling bonds? How does the bond-holder benefit from purchasing bonds?
9. *Have you or has someone you know ever purchased bonds? *Describe the experience.
10. *In your present financial situation, would the purchase of stocks or bonds be a wise investment? *Why or why not?

★★ **B. Circle the letter of the answer that best completes each of the sentences below.**

1. The process of acquiring capital is known as:
   a. accounting
   b. capitalizing
   c. financing
   d. incorporating

2. The unit of ownership in a corporation is a:
   a. bond
   b. share
   c. certificate
   d. stock

3. All corporations receive their starting capital by:
   a. selling bonds
   b. purchasing stock
   c. purchasing shares
   d. selling stock

4. The sale of corporate bonds is an example of _____ financing.
   a. debt
   b. bond
   c. equity
   d. corporate

5. A corporation may be forced to sell its assets if it does not:
   a. pay dividends
   b. share its profits with stockholders
   c. make the required payments to bondholders
   d. sell bonds

Vocabulary Exercises

★★ **A. Write down any terms that you did not understand in the reading. Find each term in the reading, look at its context, and try to figure out the meaning. Discuss these terms with your classmates.**

★   **B.** Look at the terms in the left-hand column and find the correct synonyms or definitions in the right-hand column. Copy the corresponding letters in the blanks.

1. _g_ interest payment (line 27)

2. _____ severe (line 20)

3. _____ obligation (line 28)

4. _____ source (line 6)

5. _____ entitle (line 9)

6. _____ periodic (line 27)

7. _____ issue (line 15)

8. _____ deadline (line 26)

9. _____ meet (line 29)

10. _____ initial (line 15)

a. satisfy

b. give one a right

c. occurring at regular times

d. extreme

e. first

f. the contract or promise that compels one to follow a certain course of action

✔ g. a sum paid for borrowing money

h. any thing or place from which something is obtained

i. a time limit for finishing something

j. print for sale or distribution

★★   **C.** Complete the sentences with the noun, verb, and adjective forms provided.

1. **consideration/considered/considerable**

a. After careful ___consideration___ by the board of directors, a decision was made to issue more shares of stock.

b. A corporation must raise a ___considerable___ amount of capital in order to purchase essential assets.

c. Before buying her new car, Nancy ___considered___ the price, the size, and the mileage.

2. **initiation/has initiated/initial**

a. My _____ impression of the applicant was not accurate.

b. Ms. Marovitz is an aggressive and competent manager; she _____ a number of new programs since joining the firm.

c. With the _____ of sick-leave benefits, employees could miss a certain amount of work due to illness without loss of pay.

3. **investment/to invest/invested**

a. Mr. Lee decided _____ $5,000 in Lyman Products, Inc.

b. Although he had researched the market carefully, he took a loss on his

_____.

c. A stockholder's _____ funds are usually not tax-deductible.

4. **acquisition/to acquire/acquired**

    a. There are numerous ways for a business _____ capital.

    b. The _____ of funds is an important aspect of financial manage-
    ment.

    c. The ability to type accurately and quickly is an _____ skill.

5. **finance/are financed/financial**

    a. _____ information is provided by income statements and bal-
    ance sheets.

    b. Some students _____ by their parents until they graduate from
    college.

    c. There are many job opportunities for individuals who major in the field of
    _____ .

Text Analysis

Look at the reading to answer these questions.

★ 1. What does each of the following refer to?

LINES	WORDS	REFERENTS
2	this capital	_____
8	this type of transaction	_____
28	these obligations	_____
29	its	_____

★★ 2. Two different connective words or phrases are used to show contrast (lines 5 and 19). Find these connectives and copy them below. Then write down the concepts that are being contrasted.

CONNECTIVES   CONCEPTS BEING CONTRASTED

a. _____   _____ / _____

b. _____   _____ / _____

3. In the reading, examples of equity and debt financing are given. What are the examples? What are the risk factors for each?

Equity Financing

    Example: *stocks* _____

    Risk Factors: _____

                      _____

Debt Financing

    Example: _____

    Risk Factors: _____

    _____

4. Two terms are defined in the reading using this form:

    definition ➔ verb *to be* ➔ known as ➔ term being defined

    Find and copy these definitions in the spaces below.

    a. *The process of acquiring this capital is* _____

        _____

        _____

    b. _____

        _____

        _____

Application

⭐⭐⭐ **Read the following situations and make recommendations for financial investment. Base your recommendations on information provided in this unit or on your own knowledge of finance.**

Situation 1:
Mr. and Mrs. Jeong are in their early sixties. They are both close to retirement. They have saved approximately $50,000 during their working years. They want to put their money in a secure investment that will provide them with a regular income. *What do you recommend?*

_____

_____

_____

Situation 2:
Susan Clairmont is in her late twenties. She is single, owns a home, and has a successful law practice. She finds that she can live very comfortably on 65 percent of her income. She is looking for an investment that will yield the highest return. *What do you recommend?*

_____

_____

_____

Situation 3:
John and Mary Huston are parents of four young children. John works as an engineer and Mary is a homemaker. They are able to save a small amount of John's salary

every month. They would like to invest this money now with the idea of using it later to help pay for the children's college education. *What do you recommend?*

_____

_____

_____

Information Transfer

CHARACTERISTICS OF STOCKS AND BONDS

Characteristic	Stocks	Bonds
Type of financial instrument	Equity	Debt
Order of claim	Dividends can be issued only after interest on all debts (including bonds) is fully paid.	Interest must be paid before any dividends on stock are issued.
Legal obligations to holders	Dividends may be varied or omitted at the discretion of the board of directors; no principal or maturity dates are involved.	Interest must be paid regularly to avoid insolvency; principal must be repaid at stated maturity date.
Rights of holders	Voting stockholders can influence management by electing members of the board of directors.	Bondholders have no voice in management as long as they receive interest payments.
Tax status	Dividends are not tax-deductible.	Interest as an expense of doing business is tax-deductible.

From *An Introduction to Contemporary Business*, fourth edition, by William Rudelius et al, © 1985 by Harcourt Brace Jovanovich, Inc. Reprinted by permission of the publisher.

Figure 1

★★   **A. Scan Figure 1 to answer these questions.**

    1. Which type of financial instrument is a bond? _____

    2. What example is given for equity financing? _____

    3. What must be paid first—interest payments or dividends? _____

       For whom is this a disadvantage? _____

4. Are stockholders guaranteed dividend payments? _____ Who decides when dividends will be paid? _____

5. Are bondholders guaranteed interest payments? _____ When must the principle be repaid? _____

6. Who has more influence on managerial decision-making—stockholders or bondholders? _____

7. Does a corporation pay taxes on interest? _____ Does a corporation pay taxes on dividends? _____

★★★ **B. Refer to Figure 1 to answer these questions.**

1. What advantages do stocks have over bonds?

_____

_____

_____

What advantages do bonds have over stocks?

_____

_____

2. If you had $10,000 to invest in a corporation, would you purchase stocks, bonds, or both? Why?

_____

_____

_____

3. As the financial manager of a well-established, successful corporation, how would you advise your company to raise capital?

_____

_____

_____

Additional Activities

1. Interview three people who have made financial investments. Find out what types of investments they made and why.

2. Find and bring into class a daily stock-market report. Discuss what information the various columns of figures provide.

3. Write a letter to an investment firm stating your financial situation and long-term goals. Ask for an investment recommendation.

Finance 5.3: ACQUIRING START-UP CAPITAL FOR A SMALL BUSINESS*

Warm-Up

1. Look at the possible sources of funds for small business start-up costs.

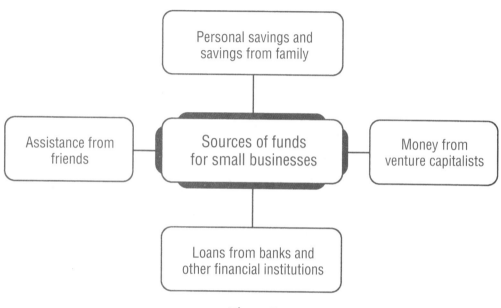

Figure 2

2. Can you think of other sources of funds for small business start-ups? If you can, add them to the graph above.
3. If you were to develop your own small business and needed $30,000 for start-up costs, which source(s) of funding would you use? Why? What are typical sources of funds for small businesses in your country?

Preparation

1. You are going to create your own small company and then apply to a local bank for start-up funds (following a simplified model). Work with a partner or in small groups to create your small business. The members of this group are the *principals* of your business. Use the following business plan to help you determine the characteristics of your business.

---

*The Small Business Administration (SBA) defines a small business as one that is independently owned and operated, not a leader in its field of operation, and meets certain standards of size and annual receipts.

BUSINESS PLAN

General information

a. Type of business (restaurant, travel agency, etc.) _____

b. Product or service _____

c. Business hours _____

d. Number of employees _____

Name of business _____

Name of owner(s) and % of ownership

_____

_____

_____

Marketing

a. Target market _____

b. Need for this good or service _____

_____

c. Major competitors _____

d. Types of promotion _____

Employees

1. Management
   a. Names and positions of key management personnel

   _____

   _____

   _____

   b. Background(s) of key management personnel

   _____

   _____

2. Workers (number and background)

   _____

   _____

Additional information relevant to your business

_____

_____

2. Now consider the financial needs of your small business.

     a. How much money is needed to start up your business?

     _____

     b. What will this money be used for (e.g., land, building(s), equipment, furniture, inventory, working capital, and advertising)?

     _____

     _____

     _____

     _____

     c. How much money do you plan to contribute from personal savings? _____ Will friends or family be lending you money for this business? If so, how much? _____ How much venture capital will there be? _____ How much will you need to borrow from the bank? _____

     Additional financial considerations: _____

     _____

     _____

     _____

     _____

Integrated Task

1. Fill out a loan application for Seaside National Bank, using the information from your business plan.

LOAN APPLICATION

Name of business _____ Date formed _____

Type of business _____

Number of employees at time of application _____

Use of proceeds:

1. Land/building(s) acquisition $ _____

2. Building construction $ _____

3. Building repair or expansion $ _____

4. Purchase of machinery and equipment $ _____

5. Purchase of furniture and fixtures $ _____

6. Inventory purchase $ _____

7. Advertising $ _____

8. Working capital $ _____

9. _____ $ _____

     TOTAL $ _____

TOTAL COST OF PROJECT: $ _____

TOTAL AMOUNT OF LOAN REQUESTED: $ _____

Name of principal _____ Telephone number _____

Position _____ ID or social security # _____

Annual salary _____ % ownership _____

Name of principal _____ Telephone number _____

Position _____ ID or social security # _____

Annual salary _____ % ownership _____

Name of principal _____ Telephone number _____

Position _____ ID or social security # _____

Annual salary _____ % ownership _____

2. Roleplay making an appointment and going to Seaside National Bank to ask for the loan. Be sure to take your business plan and the loan application. Another student in the class will roleplay the bank's loan officer. He or she will listen to you explain about your new small business, ask you some clarification questions, and then make a decision whether or not to grant your business the loan.

Possible questions the loan officer might ask the prospective borrower include:

- Can you describe your product or service in detail?
- What is the average price of this product or service?
- What are the company's goals?
- How do you plan to market this business?

Follow-Up

1. Visit a local bank to get an information packet on business loans.
2. Videotape the meeting(s) at the Seaside National Bank. Watch the videotape and make a list of effective negotiating strategies.
3. Write a cover letter to accompany your loan application. In the letter, highlight why you think your proposed small business will be successful.
4. If you are in the United States, visit a local branch of the Small Business Administration to see what kinds of services are available through the SBA.

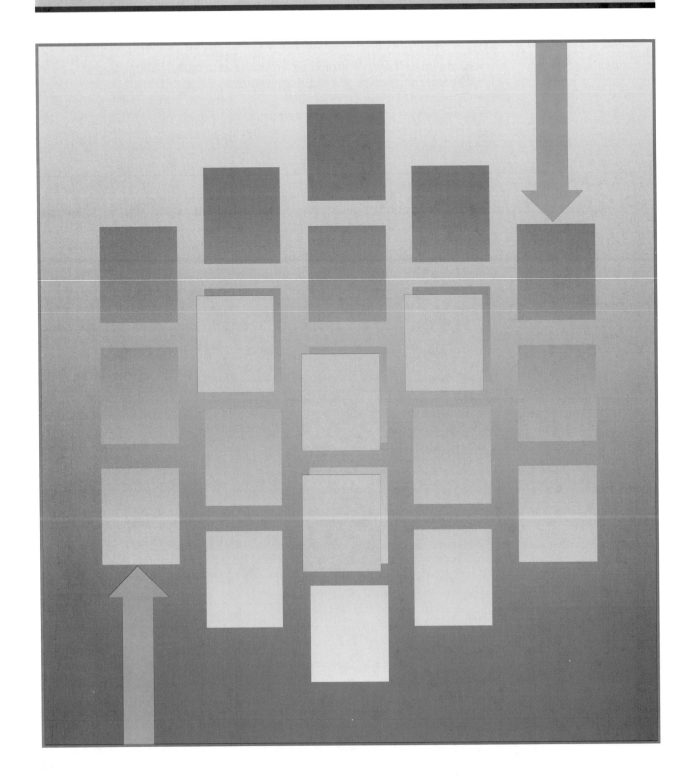

Human Aspects of Business Organizations

6. Management

6.1 Management Functions

6.2 Management and Human Resources Development

6.3 Looking at Leadership Styles

7. Decision Making

7.1 Steps in the Decision Process

7.2 The Reality of Decision Making

7.3 Deciding Who Decides

6. *Management*

Management 6.1: MANAGEMENT FUNCTIONS

Prereading Activity

Discuss the following questions.

1. What do you think of when you see the term *management*? Quickly write down words or ideas as they come into your mind.

   supervise, boss, responsibility,

2. What are some of the duties and responsibilities of a manager?

3. Have you ever worked under the supervision of a manager? Was this person an effective manager? Why or why not?

_____

_____

_____

_____

Vocabulary

Below is a list of terms that you will find in the text. As you read "Management Functions," see if you understand each term. Use this as a working list and add other terms that you do not know.

NOUNS	VERBS	ADJECTIVES	OTHERS
management	fit into	overall	regardless of
team	establish	organizational	adequately
manager	move on	ongoing	
function	revise	interpersonal	_____
position	allocate		
staffing	attain	_____	_____
direction	guide		
supervision	motivate	_____	_____
phase			
	_____	_____	
_____			
	_____		
_____			
	_____		
_____			

Reading

MANAGEMENT FUNCTIONS

Management plays a vital role in any business or organized activity. Management is composed of a team of managers who have charge of the organization at all levels. Their duties include making sure company objectives are met and seeing that the business operates efficiently. Regardless of the specific
5   job, most managers perform four basic functions:

- planning
- organizing
- directing
- controlling

10   Planning involves determining overall company objectives and deciding how these goals can best be achieved. Managers evaluate alternative plans before choosing a specific course of action and then check to see that the chosen plan fits into the objectives established at higher organizational levels. Planning is listed as the first management function because the others depend on it.
15   However, even as managers move on to perform other managerial functions, planning continues as goals and alternatives are further evaluated and revised.

Organizing, the second management function, is the process of putting the plan into action. This involves allocating resources, especially human resources, so that the overall objectives can be attained. In this phase, managers decide on
20   the positions to be created and determine the associated duties and responsibilities. Staffing, choosing the right person for the right job, may also be included as part of the organizing function.

Third is the day-to-day direction and supervision of employees. In directing, managers guide, teach, and motivate workers so that they reach their potential
25   abilities and at the same time achieve the company goals that were established in the planning process. Effective direction, or supervision, by managers requires ongoing communication with employees.

In the last management function, controlling, managers evaluate how well company objectives are being met. In order to complete this evaluation, man-
30   agers must look at the objectives established in the planning phase and at how well the tasks assigned in the directing phase are being completed. If major problems exist and goals are not being achieved, then changes need to be made in the company's organizational, or managerial, structure. In making changes, managers might have to go back and replan, reorganize, and redirect.

35   In order to adequately and efficiently perform these management functions, managers need interpersonal, organizational, and technical skills. Although all four functions are managerial duties, the importance of each may vary, depending on the situation. Effective managers meet the objectives of the company through a successful combination of planning, organizing, directing, and controlling.

Comprehension

A. **Answer the following questions about management functions. Questions with asterisks (*) cannot be answered directly from the text.**

★

1. What do the duties of managers include?
2. What does planning involve?
3. Why is planning the first management function?
4. What do managers do in the organizing phase?
5. Can staffing be considered as part of the organizing function? *Why or why not?

★★

6. *Why is ongoing communication necessary for effective direction?
7. What do managers evaluate in the controlling function? *Why is evaluation essential at this phase of a project?
8. *What types of problems could a manager discover in performing the controlling function?
9. Which skills do managers need to perform effectively? *Why is each important?
10. *Give examples of the qualities of an effective manager. *Classify these as either interpersonal, organizational, or technical skills.

★★★

B. **Complete the diagram below by writing in the management functions. Then answer the questions.**

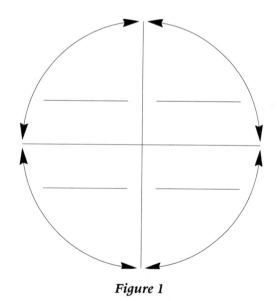

Figure 1

1. How does this circular arrangement illustrate the relationships between the four management functions?
2. Why are the arrows two-way rather than just one-way?
3. When does this cycle of planning, organizing, directing, and controlling end?
4. Are there other ways that the four management functions can be represented graphically? Draw and explain other figures.
5. Discuss and compare Figure 1 with those figures drawn by your classmates.

Vocabulary Exercises

★★ **A.** Substitute appropriate terms for the italicized words or phrases in the following sentences.

established	functions	guide	✔ team	positions
phases	allocate	attained	move on	overall

1. Often a *group* of managers, rather than an individual, works on a particular project. _____team_____

2. Plans *set up* in the first stage are subject to revision throughout the duration of the project. _____

3. Managers should periodically check to see how well *comprehensive* company goals detailed in the planning phase are being met. _____

4. Organizational goals generally are *achieved* by successfully combining the functions of planning, organizing, directing, and controlling. _____

5. It is possible to divide the organizing function into two *stages*: determining positions and their associated duties and then staffing those positions. _____

6. In order to *apportion* human resources properly, managers compare company objectives with the available resources. _____

7. Classified advertisements in newspapers and professional journals provide a list of *jobs* that are available, a brief description of each job, and a telephone number or an address. _____

8. One of the roles of a supervisor is to *direct* workers in order to maximize their talents and increase their efficiency. _____

★★ **B.** Discuss the following questions with a partner. In giving your answers, try to use the italicized terms.

1. During which management *phase* are *overall organizational* objectives *established*?
2. What personal qualities do you think good *managers* should have?
3. Which of the four *management functions* do you think is the most important? Why?
4. Why are *interpersonal* skills essential for effective *management*?
5. Why is *staffing* considered an *ongoing* managerial duty?

★★★ **C.** Fill in the blanks with the most appropriate terms from the list.

direction	adequately	manager	motivate	supervision
guided	✔ revised	interpersonal	regardless	attain

Since 1950, American manufacturing industries have _____revised_____ the _____ of their operating philosophies at the level of the manufacturing unit. As the degree of education and technical sophistication of the labor

force has increased, top management teams have _____ the established patterns of _____ to increase _____ communica-
tion from a one-way control mode to a two-way dialogue mode. In order to
_____ production targets, plant managers and supervisors realized
the need to _____ _____ the workers under their
direction.

Text Analysis

Look at the reading to answer these questions.

★ 1. What does each of the following refer to?

LINES	WORDS	REFERENTS
3	their	_____
11	these goals	_____
18	this	_____
24	they	_____

★★ 2. In line 15, a connective word is used to show a contrast. Find the connective word
and copy it below. Then write down the two concepts that are being contrasted.

_____   _____ / _____
(connective)   (concepts being contrasted)

3. What connective words or phrases, if any, are used to introduce the four basic
management functions? If no connective is used, indicate this with Ø.

CONNECTIVE WORDS OR PHRASES   MANAGEMENT FUNCTIONS

a. _____ → _____

b. *the second management function* → *organizing*

c. _____ → _____

d. _____ → _____

4. Write definitions for the management functions by matching a function on the left
with a definition on the right. Use this definition form:

term being defined → verb *to be* → definition

FUNCTIONS   DEFINITIONS

a. Planning   the day-to-day direction and supervision of workers
b. Organizing   the evaluation of how well company objectives are being met
c. Directing   the determination of overall company objectives and how they
                     can best be achieved
d. Controlling   the process of putting the plan into action

a. *Planning is* _____

_____

b. _____

_____

c. _____

_____

d. _____

_____

Writing

★★★   1. Read the following memo as if you were a member of the senior planning staff.

MEMORANDUM

TO: All Senior Planning Staff

FROM: Thomas Edwards, Vice President
               Office of Corporate Planning

DATE: June 17, 1993

SUBJECT: Proposed changes to annual corporate planning process

Present policy dictates that the three phases of the annual corporate plan be completed by the first of December each year. In order to allow more time for external document review, the following changes have been suggested.

PHASE	ITEM	PRESENT DEADLINE DATE	PROPOSED DATE
I	Initial department draft	September 1	August 1
II	Revisions by Senior Planning Staff	October 1	September 1
III	Presentation of final draft to Board of Directors for review	November 1	October 1

These proposed changes will no doubt impact your present work procedures, staffing levels, and planning methods. Your comments and suggestions are now being solicited and must be made in writing to this office no later than July 10.

TE: br

2. Prepare a response to Mr. Edwards specifically in the area of deadline dates and their effect on your staff (e.g., work procedures).

MEMORANDUM

TO: _____

FROM: _____

DATE: _____

SUBJECT: _____

_____

_____

_____

_____

_____

_____

_____

_____

_____

_____

_____

_____

_____

_____

_____

_____

_____

_____

_____

_____

Information Transfer

There are different levels of managers within the managerial hierarchy of an organization. The amount of time and effort spent on each of the four functions depends on the manager's position in the organization.

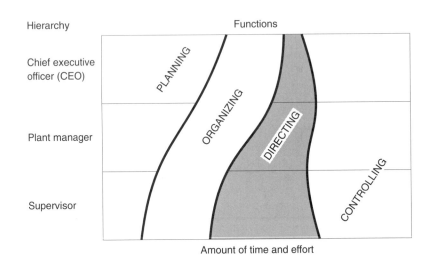

From *Supervision: Concepts and Practices of Management*, fifth edition, by Theo Haimann and Raymond L. Hilgert, copyright © 1991 by South-Western Publishing Co. Reprinted by permission of the publisher.

Figure 2

★★   A. Scan Figure 2 to answer these questions.

1. Which function(s) does the CEO spend the most time on?

   _____

2. Which function(s) does the plant manager spend the most time on?

   _____

3. Which function(s) does the supervisor spend the most time on?

   _____ The least? _____

4. In general, which function occupies the most time and effort of managers at all levels?

   _____ Why? _____

5. At which level of the hierarchy does directing occupy the most time?

   _____ Why? _____

★★★ B. Refer to Figure 2 to answer these questions.

1. Which function seems to be performed the most uniformly throughout the
hierarchy? _____

Why? _____

2. Why does the amount of time and effort spent on the directing function
decrease going from supervisor to plant manager to CEO?

_____

3. Have you ever worked as a supervisor, plant manager, or CEO? What percentage
of your time did you spend on each of the four basic management functions.

_____

Additional Activities

1. Interview a supervisor or manager to find out how much time is spent performing
each of the basic management functions. Compare the results of the interview
with your classmates.
2. Read and discuss management case studies. For example, Lawrence R. Jauch et al.
Managerial Experience: Cases, Exercises, and Readings, fifth edition (New York: Dryden
Press, 1989).
3. Ask a worker and a supervisor what kinds of skills they think an effective manager
should have. Classify the responses as interpersonal, organizational, or technical
skills. Compare the answers of the worker and the supervisor.

Management 6.2: *MANAGEMENT AND HUMAN RESOURCES DEVELOPMENT*

Prereading Activity

Discuss the following questions.

1. Directing workers is one of the functions of a manager. Have you ever been responsible for directing workers? Describe your experience.

_____

_____

_____

_____

_____

2. What can a manager do to encourage efficient and effective worker performance?

_____

_____

_____

3. When you are working for someone, what motivates you to work harder?

_____

_____

_____

Vocabulary

Below is a list of terms that you will find in the text. As you read "Management and Human Resources Development," see if you understand each term. Use this as a working list and add other terms that you do not know.

NOUNS	VERBS	ADJECTIVES	OTHERS
utilization	reveal	aware	thus
motivation	relate to	fundamental	toward
stimulus	adopt	material	likely
morale	assume	innovative	
dissatisfaction	rotate	_____	_____
maintenance	assemble	_____	_____
self-realization	_____	_____	_____
authority	_____		
_____	_____		
_____			
_____			

Reading

MANAGEMENT AND HUMAN RESOURCES DEVELOPMENT

Managers perform various functions, but one of the most important and least understood aspects of their job is proper utilization of people. Research reveals that worker performance is closely related to motivation; thus keeping employees motivated is an essential component of good management. In a busi-
5 ness context, motivation refers to the stimulus that directs the behavior of work-ers toward the company goals. In order to motivate workers to achieve company goals, managers must be aware of their needs.

Many managers believe workers will be motivated to achieve organizational goals by satisfying their fundamental needs for material survival. These needs
10 include a good salary, safe working conditions, and job security. While absence of these factors results in poor morale and dissatisfaction, studies have shown that their presence results only in maintenance of existing attitudes and work performance. Although important, salary, working conditions, and job security do not provide the primary motivation for many workers in highly industrial-
15 ized societies, especially at the professional or technical levels.

Increased motivation is more likely to occur when work meets the needs of individuals for learning, self-realization, and personal growth. By responding to personal needs—the desire for responsibility, recognition, growth, promotion, and more interesting work—managers have altered conditions in the workplace
20 and, consequently, many employees are motivated to perform more effectively.

In an attempt to appeal to both the fundamental *and* personal needs of workers, innovative management approaches, such as job enrichment and job enlargement, have been adopted in many organizations. Job enrichment gives workers more authority in making decisions related to planning and doing their
25 work. A worker might assume responsibility for scheduling work flow, checking quality of work produced, or making sure deadlines are met. Job enlargement increases the number of tasks workers perform by allowing them to rotate posi-tions or by giving them responsibility for doing several jobs. Rather than assem-bling just one component of an automobile, factory workers might be grouped
30 together and given responsibility for assembling the entire fuel system.

By improving the quality of work life through satisfaction of fundamental and personal employee needs, managers attempt to direct the behavior of work-ers toward the company goals.

Comprehension

A. Answer the following questions about management and the development of human resources. Questions with asterisks (*) cannot be answered directly from the text.

★
1. Why is it important to have employees who are motivated?
2. What is the meaning of motivation in the workplace?

3. How do many managers believe workers are motivated?
4. What happens when fundamental needs are not satisfied?

★★ 5. For which workers is satisfaction of fundamental needs not a primary motivation? *Why do you think this is true?

6. When does increased motivation generally occur for professional or technical workers?

7. What are some personal needs? *Which one do you consider the most important? *Why?

8. Why have job enrichment and job enlargement been adopted as management approaches in many organizations? *Do you view them as effective approaches? *Explain.

9. What is job enrichment? *Which personal needs does this management approach appeal to?

10. *If you were the manager of a unit that assembled pocket calculators, how might you incorporate job enrichment or job enlargement in order to increase workers' motivation?

★★ B. Determine which of the following statements are *true* and which are *false*. Then put *T* or *F* in the blanks. Rewrite false statements to make them true.

1. __*T*__ There is a close relationship between worker performance and motivation.

2. _____ In highly industrialized societies satisfaction of fundamental needs results in motivated employees who work more effectively.

3. _____ The desire for more interesting work is a fundamental need.

4. _____ A manager using the job enlargement approach might consider rotating employees.

5. _____ Managers attempt to improve the quality of work life through satisfaction of fundamental and personal employee needs.

Vocabulary Exercises

★★ A. Write down any terms that you did not understand in the reading. Find each term in the reading, look at its context, and try to figure out the meaning. Discuss these terms with your classmates.

★★ B. Look at the words in the left-hand column and find the correct synonyms or definitions in the right-hand column. Copy the corresponding letters in the blanks.

1. __*d*__ thus (line 3)   a. new; different

2. _____ stimulus (line 5)   b. the fulfillment of one's potential capacities

3. _____ material (line 9)   c. essential; necessary

4. _____ aware (line 7)   ✔ d. consequently

5. _____ morale (line 11)   e. put together

6. _____ fundamental (line 9)   f. conscious

7. _____ self-realization (line 17)　g. physical rather than spiritual or intellectual

8. _____ assemble (line 30)　h. the mental condition of an individual or group

9. _____ rotate (line 27)　i. something that causes a response

10. _____ innovative (line 22)　j. systematically alternate

★　C. Complete the sentences with the noun and verb forms provided.

1. **maintenance/to maintain**

   a. *Maintenance* _____ of the current high productivity level was a challenging goal for the factory supervisor.

   b. When the employee was transferred to a different part of the country, it became difficult for him _____*to maintain*_____ close ties with his former co-workers.

2. **assumption/assumed**

   a. The _____ that most workers are highly motivated by a good salary has been proved false.

   b. When the employee did not come to work for three weeks and failed to contact his employer, the employer _____ that he had quit.

3. **rotation/rotated**

   a. The three workers _____ positions so that each one could perform a variety of tasks.

   b. Some workers do not want to participate in job _____ because it interferes with their established routines.

4. **utilization/utilize**

   a. Managers _____ various techniques to encourage employees to work more effectively.

   b. The proper _____ of resources—both fiscal and human—is an important managerial responsibility.

5. **adoption/has adopted**

   a. The company _____ a new policy regarding sick leave.

   b. The factory manager's _____ of a new management approach resulted in increased production.

Text Analysis

Look at the reading to answer these questions.

★★ 1. What does each of the following refer to?

LINES	WORDS	REFERENTS
7	their	_____
9	these needs	_____
11	these factors	_____
12	their	_____

2. Match the connective words or phrases with the appropriate functions.

_____ but (line 1)   a. showing a result
       although (line 13)

_____ thus (line 3)   b. contrasting
       consequently (line 20)

★★★ 3. The reading discusses two kinds of worker needs and provides examples to explain them. List each need and three examples below.

Need: _____   Need: _____

Examples: _____   Examples: _____

_____   _____

_____   _____

4. Two terms are defined in the reading using this form:

   term being defined ➔ verb ➔ definition

   Find and copy these definitions in the spaces below.

   a. *Job enrichment gives* _____

   _____

   b. _____

   _____

5. Change the semiformal definitions to formal definitions. Use this form:

   term being defined ➔ verb *to be* ➔ class ➔ $\begin{Bmatrix} \text{that} \\ \text{which} \end{Bmatrix}$ ➔ definition

   a. *Job enrichment is a management approach that* _____

   _____

   b. _____

   _____

Classification

★★★ In lines 21–30 job enrichment and job enlargement are described and illustrated. Decide which management approach the following descriptions and examples represent. Then write an *X* in the correct column.

	JOB ENRICHMENT	JOB ENLARGEMENT
1. Workers check quality of work produced.	*x*	
2. Workers rotate positions.		
3. Workers are given more authority.		
4. Workers schedule work flow.		
5. Workers are responsible for assembling an entire fuel system of a car.		
6. Workers help plan their work.		
7. Workers perform a greater number of tasks.		
8. Workers make sure deadlines are met.		

Application

★★★ Discuss the information provided in Figure 3. Then divide into two groups to rank the job conditions.

HOW MANAGERS AND WORKERS RATED TEN JOB CONDITIONS

Job Conditions	Workers' Rating	Managers' Rating
Full appreciation for work done	1st	8th
Feeling "in" on things	2nd	10th
Sympathetic understanding of personal problems	3rd	9th
Job security	4th	2nd
Good wages	5th	1st
Interesting work	6th	5th
Promotion and growth with company	7th	3dr
Management loyalty to workers	8th	6th
Good working conditions	9th	4th
Tactful disciplining	10th	7th

From *Management of Organizational Behaviors Utilizing Human Resources*, fifth edition, by Paul Hersey and Kenneth Blanchard. Copyright © 1988 by Prentice-Hall Inc. Reprinted by permission of Prentice-Hall.

Figure 3

Group 1: Workers

As workers, which three job conditions would you rank as most important? Which three are least important to you as workers? Work as a group to develop one set of responses.

_____

_____

_____

Group 2: Managers

As managers, which three job conditions do you think workers consider the most important? Which three do you think they consider the least important? Work as a group to develop one set of responses.

_____

_____

_____

Compare the responses of both groups.

Now, work alone or with people of your nationality to rank the job conditions as you think workers and managers would rank them in your country. Compare your results with those of your classmates.

Additional Activities

1. Interview a supervisor or worker who is involved in an innovative management program. Find out the advantages and disadvantages of this program.
2. Find and bring to class information explaining Maslow's hierarchy of needs. Discuss how this hierarchy could be applied to a supervisor/subordinate relationship.
3. Read about and discuss McGregor's Theory X and Theory Y and Ouchi's Theory Z management assumptions. Roleplay these three types of managers as they direct workers.

Management 6.3: *LOOKING AT LEADERSHIP STYLES*

Warm-up

1. Look at the various factors influencing leadership style.

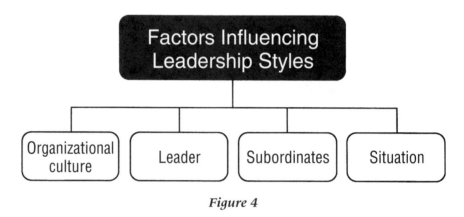

Figure 4

2. How do you think leadership style is influenced by each of the four factors listed in the chart? Try to give specific examples.
3. Can you think of other factors that affect leadership style? If so, what are they?

Preparation

1. Three broad categories of leadership styles are shown. Match each style with a definition by writing the correct number below the leadership style.

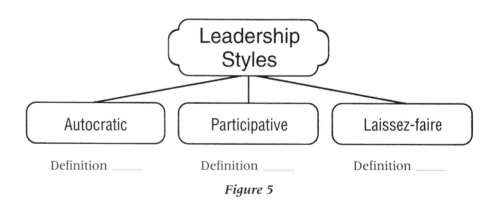

Figure 5

Definition 1: a leadership style in which the leader encourages a free flow of communication and shares decisions with the group. There is a high concern for both people and task.

Definition 2: a leadership style characterized by a "leave it alone" or "hands off" approach. The manager leads by acting mainly as a consultant and turns most decisions over to the group. There is a low concern for people and task.

Definition 3: a leadership style in which the leader uses authority in a straightforward manner by simply issuing orders. There is a high concern for the task and a low concern for people.

2. What kind of leader (autocratic, participative, or laissez-faire) might make the following statements?

   a. Mary Jones: "I prefer to hand my workers the task and let them figure out the best way to solve the problem." _____

   b. Frank Allegany: "I decide what should be done and how it should be done." _____

   c. Geraldo Gonzalez: "I try to get the opinions of all the members of the group so that we will have a consensus on the best approach." _____

3. Think of a situation in which you played a leadership role, for example, as manager of a project at work, as a teenager taking care of younger brothers and sisters, or as president of a club at school. Answer the following questions about your leadership role in that particular situation. Then discuss your answers with a partner.

A LEADERSHIP EXPERIENCE

Situation _____

Your leadership role _____

Date of event(s) _____

1. What activity did you need to direct your subordinates to accomplish? _____

2. How many subordinates were there? _____

3. Who set the objective(s)? _____

4. Who determined how you would accomplish the objective(s)? _____

5. How did you motivate your group (or did they motivate themselves)? _____

   _____

6. Was there any disagreement (conflict) in your group? If so, how did you resolve it?

   _____

   _____

7. How would you characterize your leadership style in this situation? _____

8. Did you meet your objective(s)? _____ Were you satisfied with the results of your

   leader ship? _____ Why or why not? _____

   _____

Integrated Task

1. You are now going to participate in a leadership simulation.
   a. Select three students to play the roles of leaders. (These three may be selected any way the class prefers, but they should be fairly outgoing students with strong communication skills.)
   b. The three leaders should leave the room. When they are outside the room, they should turn to Appendix A on page 180 and read their instructions.
   c. Students who remain in the classroom will divide into three groups. In a few moments the three leaders will return to the classroom. Each of the three leaders will meet with a group for about ten minutes. After each leader's session, group members will fill out the feedback form below.
   d. Study the form below while you are waiting for the three leaders to return.

LEADERSHIP EVALUATION FORM		SESSION 1	SESSION 2	SESSION 3
Did you feel included by this leader?	Yes			
	So-so			
	No			
Were you motivated to participate in this project?	Yes			
	So-so			
	No			
How would you rate this leader's overall effectiveness?	Good			
	OK			
	Weak			
What kind of leadership style do you think this leader demonstrated?	Autocratic			
	Participative			
	Laissez-faire			

2. In each group, compile your answers for the four questions on the feedback form. Then have one representative from each group share his or her group's reactions with the class. Compare the completed feedback forms of the three groups. What generalizations can you make?

3. As a class, discuss the following questions. What is the best leadership style? Do you think there is one best leadership style? Why or why not?

Follow-up

1. Form small groups and choose one leadership style to discuss. Make a list of the advantages and disadvantages of the leadership style your group chose. Present this information to the rest of the class, using the blackboard or an overhead projector.

2. Think of the leader you respect most. It can be someone in politics, religion, business, or any other field. Analyze this person's general leadership style. Why is he or she an effective leader? Write a description of this person's leadership style, including examples to support your generalizations.

3. Can you think of leadership styles other than the three discussed here? If so, what are they? Discuss the leadership style(s) commonly found in your country. Does the culture of your country influence the leadership style? If yes, how?

4. Ask five people who are not in your class the following question: Do you think good leadership skills are something a person must be born with or can the skills be acquired? Summarize the results of your survey.

7. *Decision Making*

Decision Making 7.1: STEPS IN THE DECISION PROCESS

Prereading Activity

Discuss the following questions.

1. What is an important decision you have made? How did you make this decision?

2. Can you think of a situation in which you or someone else made a poor choice? Why do you think people make poor choices?

_____

_____

_____

3. What qualities or skills should a good decision maker have? Do you think these qualities or skills are natural or can they be learned?

_____

_____

_____

Vocabulary

Below is a list of terms that you will find in the text. As you read "Steps in the Decision Process," see if you understand each term. Use this as a working list and add other terms that you do not know.

NOUNS	VERBS	ADJECTIVES	OTHERS
alternative	evaluate	ideal	somewhat
framework	state	valid	quite
expectation	experience	reliable	
incentive	schedule	feasible	_____
limitation	rely on		_____
expenditure	replace	_____	_____
implementation	guarantee	_____	
_____	_____		
_____	_____		
_____	_____		

Reading

STEPS IN THE DECISION PROCESS

One of the most important tasks a manager performs is decision making. This may be defined as the process of choosing a course of action (when alternatives are available) to solve a particular problem. The steps listed below provide a simplified framework of the ideal decision-making process:

THE DECISION-MAKING PROCESS

Define problem	Define expectation	Gather data	Develop alternatives	Evaluate alternatives	Choose best alternative
Step 1	Step 2	Step 3	Step 4	Step 5	Step 6

Figure 1

5   The first step, defining the problem, is perhaps the most difficult step. It involves careful analysis of a situation in order to state the problem and determine its cause. For example, a factory may be experiencing low production (the problem) because the supervisor has failed to schedule the work shifts in the most efficient manner (the cause).

10   Defining the expectation in Step 2 involves stating the result that is expected once the problem has been solved. The expected result after solving the problem of low production described above would be to increase the output of the factory.

Next, data are gathered about the problem. This information can be
15   obtained from a variety of sources: observations, surveys, or published research. Most businesses rely on computers to process, summarize, and report data. Having sufficient data that are valid and reliable is necessary for Step 4.

Here the decision maker develops feasible alternatives, or potential solu-
20   tions, to the problem. Using the low production example, some alternatives might include the following:

- replacing the current supervisor
- providing the current supervisor with the necessary information and training to schedule the work shifts more efficiently
25   - creating incentives for workers, such as higher pay or time off, in order to increase production

In the fifth step, the decision maker evaluates these alternatives in terms of the expected result of the solution (which is to increase production) and limitations, such as time and money. The first alternative, replacing the current
30   supervisor, does not guarantee increased production, and it would involve training a new supervisor. The second alternative, providing additional training for the current supervisor, would be time-consuming and somewhat expensive but should bring about increased production. The last alternative, creating worker incentives, may bring about increased production but would be quite
35   expensive.

Finally, the decision maker compares the alternatives and chooses the one that has the best potential for providing the desired results. In the low production example, the decision maker decides to try providing the current supervisor with additional training because this alternative should achieve the objective with the lowest expenditure of time and money.

40

The decision-making process is followed by:

- implementation of the chosen alternative (putting it into action)
- evaluation of that alternative

If the alternative achieves the desired result, it is then known as the solution.

Comprehension

★★ **A. Answer the following questions about the decision-making process. Questions with asterisks (*) cannot be answered directly from the text.**

1. What is decision making? *Why does the definition include "when alternatives are available"?
2. What are the six steps of the ideal decision-making process? *How does the decision-making process that you described in the Prereading Activity compare to the ideal model?
3. Defining the problem involves two steps. What are they?
4. What is the expected result after solving the problem of low production?
5. Where can data be obtained?
6. What does the decision maker do after obtaining data? *Why must the alternatives be "feasible"?
7. How does the decision maker evaluate the alternatives?
8. Why was the second alternative in the problem of low production chosen? *Do you think it was the best choice? *Why or why not?
9. What follows the six steps outlined in the decision-making process? *Do you think evaluation is always necessary? *Explain.

★★ **B. Determine which of the following statements are _true_ and which are _false_. Then put T or F in the blanks. Rewrite false statements to make them true.**

1. __T__ Defining the problem can be one of the most difficult steps in the decision-making process.

2. _____ Computers provide valuable support for decision makers.

3. _____ Another feasible alternative in the problem of low production might be to replace all the factory workers.

4. _____ Time and money are considered in the evaluation of alternatives.

5. _____ The alternative selected in Step 6 always solves the problem.

Vocabulary Exercises

★ **A.** Look at the terms in the left-hand column and find the correct synonyms or definitions in the right-hand column. Copy the corresponding letters in the blanks.

1. __e__ reliable (line 17)	a. choice; option
2. ____ feasible (line 19)	b. encouragement; stimulus
3. ____ state (line 6)	c. provide a substitute for
4. ____ alternative (line 2)	d. declare; set forth in words
5. ____ framework (line 4)	✔ e. dependable
6. ____ incentive (line 25)	f. possible
7. ____ ideal (line 4)	g. structure
8. ____ replace (line 22)	h. existing only in the mind; often not real or practical

★★★ **B.** Discuss the following questions with a partner. In giving your answers, try to use the italicized terms.

1. What are some *incentives* governments provide to encourage business and investments?
2. What kinds of *limitations* does the government place on business in your country? Do you favor these kinds of restrictions?
3. Many products nowadays are *guaranteed* to be of satisfactory quality. Have you ever purchased a product that was *guaranteed*? Explain.
4. What *expectations* do you have for your future career? Do you think these *expectations* are *feasible*?
5. Do you usually make personal decisions on your own or do you *rely on* someone else for advice?

★★★ **C.** Fill in the blanks below with the most appropriate terms from the list.

evaluate	alternatives	✔ rely on	validity	reliable
ideal	limitations	guarantee	replace	expenditure

Decision makers ____*rely on*____ data to develop potential solutions to a problem; therefore, the accumulation of _____ data is an important aspect of the decision-making process. Decision makers _____ their data to make sure that the information is indeed valid. _____ may be determined by age of data, size of the statistical sample, methods used to obtain the data, and so forth. There are _____ as to how much time and money a decision maker can devote to gathering data, so the _____ of time and money is determined by the importance of the problem. Although the accumulation and analysis of reliable data are prerequisites for the development of feasible _____ to a problem, having reliable data does not, unfortunately, _____ that a solution will be found.

Text Analysis

Look at the reading to answer these questions.

★

1. What does each of the following refer to?

LINES	WORDS	REFERENTS
5	it	_____
19	here	_____
36	one	_____
39	this alternative	_____

★★

2. List the six steps of the decision-making process in correct order.

- developing alternatives
- defining the expectation
- choosing the best alternative
- gathering data
- defining the problem
- evaluating alternatives

a. _____

b. _____

c. _____

d. _____

e. _____

f. _____

3. Connective or key words and phrases are used to introduce each of the six steps in the decision-making process. What are these connectives?

CONNECTIVES		STEPS
a. *the first step*	→	*defining the problem*
b. _____	→	_____
c. _____	→	_____
d. _____	→	_____
e. _____	→	_____
f. _____	→	_____

4. The problem of a factory experiencing low production is discussed in the reading. In Step 4, three alternatives, or potential solutions to this problem, are developed. List them below. In Step 5, these alternatives are evaluated in terms of (1) effects on production and (2) limitations such as time and money. Write the information that is provided for each alternative regarding production and limitations.

ALTERNATIVES	EFFECTS ON PRODUCTION	LIMITATIONS
a. *replacing current supervisor*	*increased production is not guaranteed*	*necessary to train a new supervisor*
b. _____	_____	_____
c. _____	_____	_____

Application

★★★ Read the situations and follow the steps in the decision-making process to solve the problems.

1. *Situation*: The productivity of a department has decreased because a subordinate is not giving a new manager the necessary support and cooperation.

Define the Problem

Problem = _____

Cause = _____

Define the Expectation

_____

Gather Data (Some have been provided; add more if necessary.)

- The company employs more than 250 people.
- The manager was hired from the outside. He has extensive experience and is interested in introducing some innovations.
- The subordinate is an older man who has been with the company many years. He is satisfied with the current systems in place. The other employees like and respect him.

_____

_____

_____

_____

Develop Alternatives

1. _____
2. _____
3. _____

Evaluate Alternatives

1. _____
2. _____
3. _____

Choose the Best Alternative

_____

2. *Situation*: Blair Accounting Services, Inc., is losing many of its valuable accountants to a competing firm that offers higher salaries and more benefits.

Define the Problem

Problem = _____

Cause = _____

Define the Expectation

_____

Gather Data (Some have been provided; add more if necessary.)

- Blair Accounting Services, Inc. is a relatively small firm, employing 60 people.
- Employees are very satisfied with their jobs, except for salaries and benefits.
- The company has recently acquired a number of new clients.
- Currently there is a shortage of qualified accountants in this region.

_____

_____

_____

Develop Alternatives

1. _____
2. _____
3. _____

Evaluate Alternatives

1. _____
2. _____
3. _____

Choose the Best Alternative

_____

Writing

★★★ Write a memorandum for one of the following situations. Use the memo format presented in Management on page 118.

Situation 1: The manager discussed on page 140 writes a memorandum to his superior explaining the problem and what was done about it.

Situation 2: The president of Blair Accounting Services, Inc. (page 141) writes a memorandum to all his employees outlining changes in salaries and personnel benefits.

MEMORANDUM

TO: _____

FROM: _____

DATE: _____

SUBJECT: _____

_____

_____

_____

_____

_____

_____

_____

_____

_____

Additional Activities

1. Develop a questionnaire and interview three people about important decisions they have made. Find out what factors influenced their decisions the most.
2. Read and apply the decision-making process to case studies, for example, Theo Haimann and Raymond L. Hilgert, *Supervision: Concepts and Practices of Management*, fifth edition (Cincinnati: South-Western Publishing Co., 1991).
3. Select a current global problem (political, social, environmental, etc.) that you would like to see solved. Find and bring to class data that might help in the solution of this problem. As a class, follow the decision-making process as outlined in this chapter.

Decision Making 7.2: *THE REALITY OF DECISION MAKING*

Prereading Activity

Discuss the following questions.

1. In making a decision, can you always follow the six steps of the ideal model that were discussed in the first reading?

_____

Give examples to explain when or why a step might have to be changed.

_____

_____

_____

2. If you were a buyer on the international market, what risks would you be willing to take by yourself? When would you consult your supervisor before making a decision? When would you make a decision on your own?

_____

_____

_____

_____

Vocabulary

Below is a list of terms that you will find in the text. As you read "The Reality of Decision Making," see if you understand each term. Use this as a working list and add other terms that you do not know.

NOUNS	VERBS	ADJECTIVES	OTHERS
reality	implement	environmental	frequently
factor	influence	relative	_____
organization	affect	practical	
background	alter	_____	_____
interaction	limit		
restriction	weigh	_____	
flexibility	tend		
creativity		_____	
risk	_____		
_____	_____		
_____	_____		

Reading

THE REALITY OF DECISION MAKING

Decision making is a complex business subject which combines the most complicated elements of the operational and theoretical aspects of management. The ability to implement the decision-making process is often determined by environmental factors rather than the steps in some "ideal" model. Decisions are

5 frequently influenced more by the environment and structure of the organization than by the method itself. The process of decision making will, therefore, be examined in light of environmental factors.

One of these factors—social and cultural background—affects the interaction among people involved in the decision process and provides the cultural

10 framework within which they may comfortably operate. The best alternative for solving a problem, for example, might be to replace an employee who is unsuited for a position. However, if in the society's culture there is a tradition of lifetime employment with one company, that alternative is not really feasible because of social and cultural restrictions.

15 With regard to the structure of an organization, a number of factors may alter the ideal decision-making process. The amount of flexibility within an organization and the available resources (such as facilities, technology, or fiscal reserves) are often controlling factors. The amount of data available may also limit the range of alternatives that can be considered. Another organizational

20 factor is the importance of the decision being made in relation to other problems and responsibilities of management. The relative importance of one decision is weighed against the amount of effort involved in finding a solution and the benefit the company will receive from its implementation.

Three other factors also influence the following of a model decision process:

25 time, creativity, and risk. The amount of time available to make a decision for a given problem is often determined by the environment, not the management. The time factor may affect the creativity of the solution to a problem. The risk associated with a particular course of action may be lessened by use of a group rather than an individual decision maker. Time, resources, and culture may

30 affect the workability of a group process, although research shows that groups often come up with better solutions than individuals.

Decision theory and the ideal decision-making model tend to picture the process as one in which managers operate by themselves, free of restrictions of time, data, and resources. The reality of the decision process is much less a step-

35 by-step procedure than it is a series of practical considerations directly influenced by the social, cultural, and organizational environment.

Comprehension

★★ A. Answer the following questions about decision making. Questions with asterisks (*) cannot be answered directly from the text.

1. What often influences the final decision?
2. How is the process of decision making examined in this reading?
3. How does social and cultural background affect the decision process?
4. How is the relative importance of a decision determined?

5. *How is creativity affected by the amount of time available to reach a decision?

6. Is risk lessened when a group, rather than an individual decision maker, takes a particular course of action ? *Why or why not?

7. *How would a manager decide whether an individual or a group should be involved in making a decision?

★★★ B. Complete the diagram below by writing in those factors that affect the decision-making environment. First, list factors that were discussed in the reading. Then write in other factors. Put in additional lines and arrows as needed.

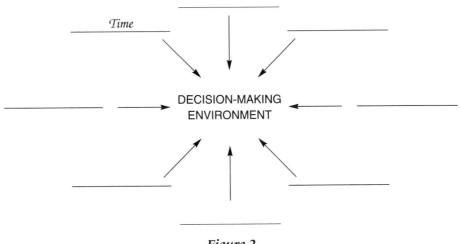

Time

DECISION-MAKING ENVIRONMENT

Figure 2

Vocabulary Exercises

★★ A. Write down any terms that you did not understand in the reading. Find each term in the reading, look at its context, and try to figure out the meaning. Discuss these terms with your classmates.

★★ B. Substitute appropriate terms for the italicized words or phrases in the following sentences.

| implement | flexibility | relative | creativity | restrictions |
| ✔ alter | reality | tend | practical | background |

1. Various factors influence and *modify* the decision-making environment.

   alter

2. Governments often place *limitations* on the types of goods that can be imported.

   _____

3. Often restricted by a lack of time, managers *are inclined* to choose what appears to be a good alternative without fully exploring other feasible alternatives.

   _____

4. Although there may be many ways to solve a problem, only some of these are *feasible*, given the social, cultural, and organizational environment. _____

5. Once a decision has been reached, it is important to *execute* the chosen alternative at the appropriate time. _____

6. To assess a business decision clearly, a manager must fully understand and deal with the *actual circumstances* of the situation. _____

7. A person's *experience, training, and education* influence creativity and risk taking.

_____

8. In developing alternatives, a decision maker uses *imagination* in order to think of new, unique potential solutions. _____

★★   C. Complete the sentences with the noun, verb, and adjective forms provided.

1. **creativity/creates/creative**

   a. Advertisers often use their _____*creative*_____ talents to design original, eye-catching promotions.

   b. Time, _____*creativity*_____, and risk are three factors that influence the decision-making process.

   c. The combination of product, price, placement, and promotion _____*creates*_____ the marketing mix.

2. **alterations/alter/alterable**

   a. Within an organization, a number of factors _____ the ideal decision-making process.

   b. Plans are often subject to slight _____ before implementation.

   c. Although the project was in the final planning phase, the director indicated that the plans were still _____.

3. **interaction/interact/interactive**

   a. Healthy _____ between employer and employee maintains open lines of communication.

   b. Some people choose to work in a highly _____ profession, such as sales.

   c. Factors surrounding and contributing to a situation _____ to shape the decision-making environment.

4. **flexibility/flexes/flexible**

   a. A manager who is _____ adapts to organizational change more easily than one who rigidly resists modification.

   b. An organization's _____ and its available resources often determine its decision process.

   c. In constructing a new children's toy, designers are looking for a material that _____ and does not break easily.

5. **influence/is influenced/influential**

   a. The shop steward frequently used his _____ to settle disagree-
      ments among the workers.

   b. The decision process within an organization _____ by a variety
      of environmental factors.

   c. Because of his education, background, and experience, he had become an
      _____ member of the business community.

Text Analysis

Look at the reading to answer these questions.

★★ 1. What does each of the following refer to?

LINES	WORDS	REFERENTS
8	these factors	_____
10	they	_____
13	that alternative	_____
35	it	_____

2. Match the connective words or phrases with the appropriate functions.

   _____ therefore (line 6)   a. contrasting

   _____ for example (line 11)   b. adding information

   _____ however (line 12)   c. summarizing

   _____ also (line 24)   d. illustrating

3. In lines 17–18, what are *facilities, technology, and fiscal reserves* examples of?

   _____

   _____

4. In line 25, what are *time, creativity, and risk* examples of?

   _____

   _____

★★★ 5. Paragraph 3 discusses the organizational factors that may affect the decision-
      making process. List those factors below.

   ORGANIZATIONAL FACTORS

   a. *amount of flexibility* _____

   b. _____

   c. _____

   d. _____

148   *Part IV*

Classification

⭐⭐⭐ Divide into small groups and discuss the following factors that affect the decision-making environment. Consider each restriction that is listed below the factors and decide whether an individual or group would make a good decision more efficiently. Write an *X* in the column under your choice. For example, if a decision were being made in a company where all the employees came from the same cultural background, would an individual decision maker or a group function better? On the other hand, if the employees came from different cultural backgrounds, which one would function better? There are no right or wrong answers for this exercise. In your discussion of these factors, give reasons and examples to support your opinions.

FACTORS	INDIVIDUAL	GROUP
1. Cultural background		
• Same	_____	_____
• Different	_____	_____
2. Organizational flexibility		
• Open to change	_____	_____
• Rigid	_____	_____
3. Available resources		
• Abundant	_____	_____
• Somewhat limited	_____	_____
4. Data		
• Large quantity	_____	_____
• Small amount	_____	_____
5. Relative importance		
• Priority decision	_____	_____
• Minor decision	_____	_____
6. Time		
• No specific deadline	_____	_____
• Limited	_____	_____
7. Creativity		
• High	_____	_____
• Low (fairly routine decision)	_____	_____
8. Risk		
• More willing to take risks	_____	_____
• Less willing to take risks	_____	_____

Information Transfer

★★★ The figure that follows is a graphic representation of the decision process known as a decision-flow diagram, or decision tree. In this particular case, a company executive's staff has done preliminary work to help determine whether the company should purchase or lease a new copying machine. The executive initially completed the first two steps in the decision process—defining the problem and examining the company's expectations. The staff gathered data, developed alternatives, and then presented these documented options. Finally, the executive must evaluate the alternatives and choose the most appropriate one.

All decisions are a combination of known facts and unknown consequences, that is, the probability of events occurring as planned or predicted. In the diagram a square ■ indicates a point, or "fork," where a decision must be made. A circle ● indicates the location of a chance, or estimate, fork—where unknown occurrences or conditions are being predicted.

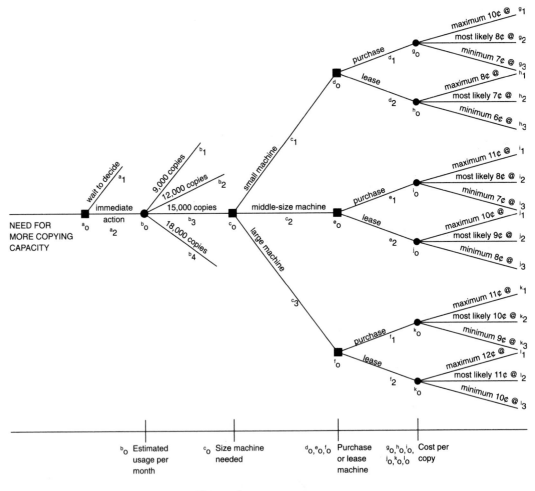

Figure 3

★★★ **A. Read page 150 and scan Figure 3 to answer these questions.**

1. What were the first two steps in the decision process through which the executive had to progress? _____

_____

2. What was the cause or situation that prompted the need for this tree?

_____

_____

3. Which locations in the diagram indicate decision points? _____

_____

4. How many chance forks does this decision tree offer? _____

_____

5. At what point in the decision-flow diagram did the first decision need to be made? _____ What was the outcome of the decision? _____ Which path, or leg, did the outcome of this decision take?

_____

6. What decision tree option does point b_0 represent? _____ Why is location b_0 a chance fork?

_____

_____

7. Given options b_1, b_2, b_3, and b_4, what eventual outcome occurred?

_____

_____

8. At point c_0, which specific decision needs to be made? _____

_____

_____

★★★ **B. Refer to Figure 3 to answer these questions.**

1. Based on cost per copy alone, would you recommend purchase of a small, medium, or large machine? _____ Why? _____

_____

Which option, or leg, of the chance fork did you select before making a final recommendation to the executive? _____

2. Using the same procedure as in the previous question, would it be most cost-effective (based solely on the unit cost per copy) to lease the small, medium, or large machine? _____

   Why? _____

   _____

   On which chance fork, or probability path, did you base your decision?

   _____

3. In Figure 3 the decision criterion has been based on only one factor, cost per unit. What other factors might influence the decision to purchase or lease a copying machine? _____

   _____

   _____

Additional Activities

1. Listen to a representative from a medium-to-large company explain the decision-making process in his or her organization.
2. Develop a questionnaire based on the factors affecting the decision-making environment (Figure 2) and interview people regarding the process of decision making where they work.
3. Draw a decision tree for either a personal or business decision you need to make. Present and discuss your example.

Decision Making 7.3: DECIDING WHO DECIDES

Warm-up

1. Look at the diagram below. It shows a typical hierarchy in a business organization.

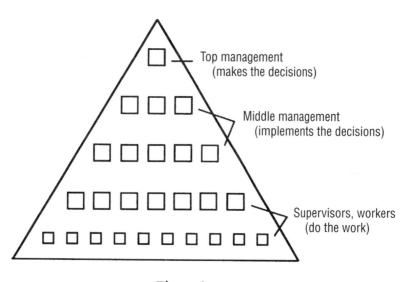

Figure 4

2. What is the role of top management in this hierarchy? Of middle management? What role do supervisors and workers play in decision making?
3. Do you think this is an effective model for the decision-making process? Can you think of other ways in which good and effective decisions are made?

Preparation

1. Circle the letter of the answer that you most agree with. (There is no one correct answer.)

    a. A good decision maker should:
       1. encourage subordinates to agree with him/her
       2. discourage all forms of disagreement
       3. allow for both agreement and disagreement in discussing various options

    b. Meetings are generally:
       1. effective if properly run
       2. a waste of time
       3. the best way to solve a problem

    c. Decisions are usually best handled by:
      1. top management
      2. all levels of management, depending on the situation
      3. everyone who works for the company

    d. People with strong decision-making skills:
      1. usually have a technical background
      2. are generally in upper management
      3. can represent a variety of backgrounds

Discuss your answers with a partner and explain why you made these particular choices.

2.   Match the terms on the left with definitions on the right.

    _____ centralization

        a. the distribution of decision-making authority throughout all levels of management by extensive delegation

    _____ decentralization

        b. the concentration of authority for most decisions at the top levels of an organization

3.   Both centralization and decentralization in the decision-making process have advantages. With a partner, write down as many advantages as you can think of for each.

ADVANTAGES OF CENTRALIZATION	ADVANTAGES OF DECENTRALIZATION
Fewer people involved; simpler	*Increased acceptance of decision*

4.   Look at and discuss the continuum of decision-making methods.

Individual decision	Consultative decision	Group decision

⟵ More centralized   Less centralized ⟶

Figure 5

Integrated Task

1. Working in small groups, read and discuss the following situation.

You work for a small company that has 14 employees. For a number of years now it has been a tradition to have an annual company dinner. Sometimes you go out to a restaurant, and other years you have had a potluck dinner at an employee's house. The following issues need to be decided for this year's dinner:

- Which restaurant or whose house
- Time and date
- Whether to include families or not
- If a potluck: • who will bring which food
                   • who will provide drinks, plates, napkins, eating utensils, etc.
                   • who will help clean up
- Additional issues to be decided? _____

_____

---

2. Which type of decision-making method would be best for this situation: individual (the general manager of the company), consultative (the general manager, incorporating the advice of certain employees), or group (the general manager and all the employees)?
3. Make the necessary decisions, using the type of process you recommended above. (The method chosen will determine the various people involved in making the decisions.) If necessary, revise your decision-making process.

Follow-up

1. Present your group's recommendations for the annual company dinner and ask for feedback from the group about the effectiveness of their decision-making process.
2. Draw a chart to represent a typical hierarchy of a small or medium-sized business organization in your country. You may use the model from page 153.
3. Discuss the decision-making process that businesses normally use in your culture. Explain where on the decision-making continuum you think business in your country falls.
4. Form small groups with students from your country or culture. Roleplay a situation in which you use the decision-making process described in Question 3 above. Videotape the various roleplays, play back the video, and analyze the different approaches.

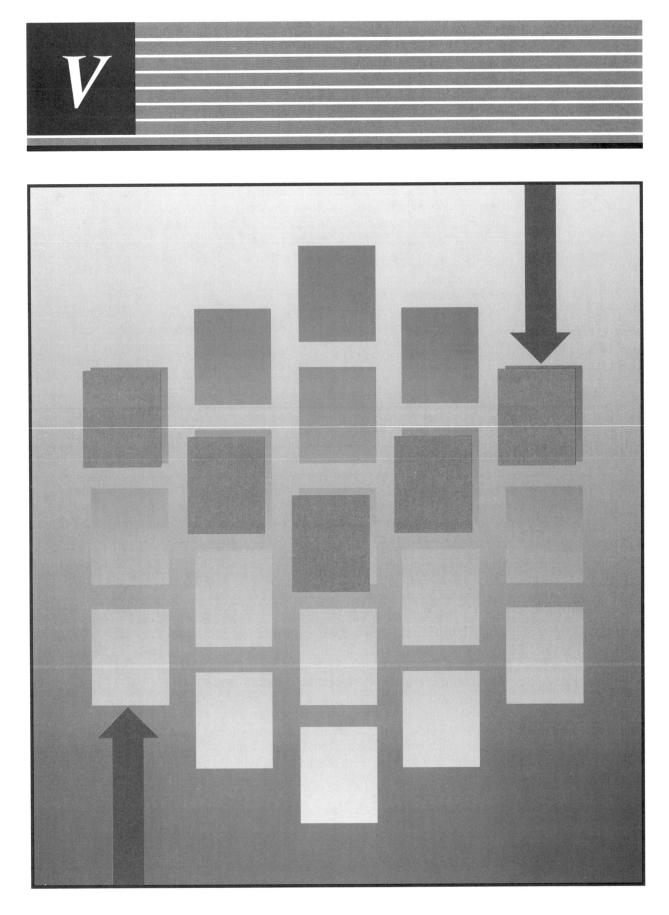

Business
and Technology

8. Computer Applications

8.1 Business Computer Systems

8.2 Expert Systems

8.3 Solving a "Stock Out" Problem

8. *Computer Applications*

Computer Applications 8.1: BUSINESS COMPUTER SYSTEMS

Prereading Activity

Discuss the following questions.

1. Do you use computers on a regular basis? Describe your experience.

2. Many companies manufacture computer hardware. What are some companies with which you are familiar?
   IBM, Apple

3. What software programs have you used (e.g., word processing and graphics programs)?

_____

_____

_____

4. If you were the manager of a local retail clothing store, how could you use computers in your daily work?

_____

_____

_____

Vocabulary

Below is a list of terms that you will find in the text. As you read "Business Computer Systems," see if you understand each term. Use this as a working list and add other terms that you do not know.

NOUNS	VERBS	ADJECTIVES	OTHERS
technology	revolutionize	high-tech	in fact
accuracy	manipulate	affordable	currently
data	store	integral	_____
data processing	print	routine	_____
tool	integrate	portable	_____
application	access	creative	
operation	simulate	_____	
role	_____	_____	
teleconferencing	_____	_____	
computer program			
chip			
_____			
_____			
_____			

Reading

BUSINESS COMPUTER SYSTEMS

Computers continue to revolutionize business. Managers, for example, use information from expert systems to help in the decision-making process, and market analysts use complex computer databases to analyze and forecast consumer behavior. In fact, computer technology is the most important aspect of the late twentieth-century information revolution. This technology has led to the development of the new high-tech industries, such as microelectronics and robotics.

Speed, a high degree of accuracy, and the ability to manipulate and store large amounts of data led to the early specialization of computers in data processing. More recently, the smaller personal computers (microcomputers) have become affordable, and software packages have been developed to support numerous business functions. Increasingly used as managerial tools, personal computers have become an integral part of many managers' offices.

Computers and their applications have resulted in more efficient and productive business operations. They perform routine functions such as payroll preparation and inventory control and more complex ones such as sales forecasting and preparation of "what if" questions for market analysis.

Computer technology is developing so rapidly that it is difficult to foresee exactly what roles computers will play in business in the future. However, numerous computer applications are currently performing vital roles in business operations. Some of these include:

- *word processing*—using the computer to create, store, edit, and print text. Examples of texts include letters, memos, reports, and other written business communications. Replacing the traditional typewriter, word processors are usually the first step in office automation.

- *networking*—the integration of computer systems, workstations, and communications links. Computer networks are designed to meet business requirements by allowing users rapid and simultaneous access to key business information. Computer applications such as electronic mail and teleconferencing are only possible in a networked computer environment.

- *database*—a collection of information that is integrated and can be accessed for a variety of business applications. In this electronic filing system, businesses can store, update, and manipulate information related to operations such as sales and customer demographics more efficiently than in older generations of computer programs (e.g., FORTRAN and COBOL).

- *spreadsheet*—a collection of numbers, formulas, and worksheets. The electronic spreadsheet contains rows and columns and is used for sales forecasts, reports, income statement and balance sheet preparation, and many other numerical analyses.

- *expert system*—a sophisticated computer program that applies specialized knowledge drawn from human experts in order to solve problems. By applying symbolic logic and a series of rules, an expert system simulates the behavior of human experts in solving problems in similar situations.

45   The increasing power and affordability of computer hardware and software have led to an even wider use of computers in business. As a result of the development of the microprocessor, which is really a computer on a chip, it is possible to have a portable electronic office. For a salesperson in the field, a computer that fits in a briefcase has quickly given way to one that can be held in the palm of the hand (palmtop). Equipped with a modem, the portable office allows instantaneous communications with the home office for solving customer problems.

50   Computer technology and software applications are providing numerous opportunities for business. The challenge is to recognize these opportunities and manage them in a creative and knowledgeable way.

Comprehension

A. **Answer the following questions about business computer systems. Questions with asterisks (*) cannot be answered directly from the text.**

★

1. What is the most important aspect of the late twentieth-century information revolution? *Why?
2. What are two examples of high-tech industries?
3. What are some of the attributes of computers that led to their early specialization in data processing? *What are some tasks that computers can perform better than human beings?
4. What five computer applications are discussed in the reading? *Have you used any of these? *Which ones?
5. Which computer application deals primarily with numbers? Which one allows computers to talk to each other?
6. Which application is usually the first step in office automation? *Have you ever used a word processing program? *Which one?

★★★

7. Which application relies on knowledge gained from experts? *Who do you think provides the best solutions to problems—human beings or computer expert systems? *Why?
8. *What are some other computer applications that are being used in business today?
9. Why are computers being used more and more widely in business?
10. *What are some of the software applications that business will use in the future?

★★ B. **Circle the letter of the answer that best completes the sentences below.**

1. _____ is not an advantage of current computer technology.
   a. accuracy
   b. ability to work with a lot of data
   c. ability to apply common sense logic
   d. speed

2. A routine business function is _____
   a. planning for a new building
   b. paying employees
   c. forecasting potential markets
   d. developing a product line

3. A/An _____ has replaced the traditional filing system.
   a. database
   b. spreadsheet
   c. word processor
   d. expert system

4. A/An _____ relies on information provided by authorities in order to solve problems.
   a. spreadsheet
   b. expert system
   c. word processor
   d. database

5. The smallest computer is a _____.
   a. modem
   b. microcomputer
   c. minicomputer
   d. palmtop

Vocabulary Exercises

★★ A. Write down any terms that you did not understand in the reading. Find each term in the reading, look at its context, and try to figure out the meaning. Discuss these terms with your classmates.

★ B. Look at the terms in the left-hand column and find the correct synonyms or definitions in the right-hand column. Copy the corresponding letters in the blanks.

1. __e__ application (line 13)   a. produce a copy on paper

2. ____ affordable (line 10)   b. change dramatically

3. ____ simulate (line 41)   c. now; at this time

4. ____ accuracy (line 7)   d. relating to habitual procedures

5. ____ role (line 18)   ✔ e. use of a theory or technique to achieve a desired outcome, e.g. a computer program

6. ____ revolutionize (line 1)   f. imitate; replicate; act like

7. ____ tool (line 11)   g. hold or keep for future use

8. ____ currently (line 19)   h. capable of being carried

9. ____ portable (line 46)   i. function

10. ____ print (line 21)   j. able to be bought fairly easily

11. ____ store (line 21)   k. correctness; having few errors

12. ____ routine (line 14)   l. method, concept, or instrument that is needed to perform a task

★   C. **Complete the sentences with the noun and verb forms provided.**

1. **integration/integrate**

   a. Some software programs _____*integrate*_____ word processing, database, and spreadsheet options.

   b. Increasingly, a manager's job involves effective _____*integration*_____ of technology and human beings.

2. **manipulation/manipulate**

   a. Because computers can _____ large amounts of data, they were first used for data processing.

   b. _____ of a text file, for example, changing the spacing or editing, is easy to do with a word processor.

3. **storage/store**

   a. Computers have become increasingly smaller with a greater _____ capacity than could have been envisioned earlier.

   b. One of the greatest advantages of computers is the ability to _____ massive amounts of information and recall it for future use.

4. **applications/applied**

   a. Computer technology is being _____ to many aspects of our daily lives.

   b. Computer _____ can be found not only in business but also in health care, entertainment, transportation, and government operations.

5. **simulations/simulate**

   a. Students in business courses often participate in _____ .

   b. An expert system is designed to _____ the decision-making process of human experts in a business environment.

Text Analysis

Look at the reading to answer these questions.

★   1. What does each of the following refer to?

LINES	WORDS	REFERENTS
14	they	_____
15	ones	_____
47	one	_____
52	them	_____

2. Match the connective words or phrases with the appropriate function.

____ for example (line 1)   a. showing cause/effect

____ in fact (line 4)   b. emphasizing

____ however (line 18)   c. contrasting

____ as a result (line 44)   d. illustrating

★★★ 3. The reading discusses various computer applications and provides examples to explain them. List each application, the word or phrase introducing the examples, and then the examples. Do not use expert system.

APPLICATION	WORD OR PHRASE	EXAMPLES
a. _____	_____	_____
b. *Networking*	_____	_____
c. _____	_____	_____
d. _____	*is used for*	_____

Classification

★★★ Read each sentence below. Determine which of the computer applications each situation is most closely related to. Write *word processing, networking, database, spreadsheet*, or *expert system* in the blank spaces.

1. A production manager calls up a list of customers who buy the company's major product line.   *database*

2. A cost accountant prepares a detailed breakdown of the costs of a new product.   _____

3. A draft of a letter is printed out and saved for further revisions.   _____

4. An Engineer turns on the computer and accesses his or her electronic mail.   _____

5. A credit card company processes applications, offering new cards to some applicants and investigating others further.   _____

6. A marketing analyst accesses information about potential market demographics.   _____

7. The parent corporation seeks and receives timely information about the sales in its various branch offices.   _____

8. A business consultant prints out a final report to give to his or her client.   _____

9. A stockbroker asks for a recommendation about whether to buy a particular stock.   _____

10. The general manager of a food processing plant asks to see the balance sheets for the last three quarters.   _____

Application

A flowchart is a pictorial representation of the sequence of steps to be performed. Computer programmers frequently use flowcharts as an initial step in the preparation of programs. The flowchart itself is not a program, nor is it written in a computer language; it merely helps the programmer determine how to arrange and write the program.

The flowchart in Figure 1 shows the sequence of steps taken in issuing airline tickets. Notice that the oval figures represent beginning and ending; the rectangular figures represent processing; and the circles indicate a point at which a decision needs to be made.

Flowchart for Issuing Airline Tickets

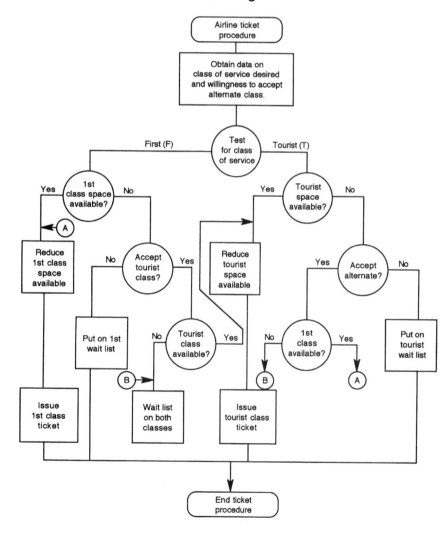

Figure from *Contemporary Business*, fourth edition, by Louis E. Boone and David L. Kurtz, copyright © 1985 by The Dryden Press, reproduced by permission of the publisher.

Figure 1

★★★ **A.** Draw a flowchart. Include as many decision-making steps as possible. Choose your own subject or use one of the following suggestions:

- applying for a credit card
- making an appointment with your supervisor
- ordering a business lunch in a restaurant
- cashing a check
- choosing a career
- choosing a good university that offers the major you want

★★★ **B.** Divide into groups according to flowchart activities; that is, sit with those people who made flowcharts of the same activity that you did. Look at everyone's flowchart and compare them.

1. Which flowchart is the most complex? Which is the least complex?
2. Which one has the most decision-making steps?
3. Which one is the most efficient?
4. Can you see any ways to improve your flowchart? How?
5. Do you think flowcharts are a useful tool in computer programming? Can you think of any other areas in which they might be helpful or useful?

Additional Activities

1. Visit a computer store. Try out some of the various software applications for personal computers.
2. Listen to a representative from a local company explain how computers are utilized in that particular business.
3. Develop a questionnaire and interview people about their perception of the role of computers in the year 2000 and beyond. Observe whether people respond with positive or negative feelings to the increasing role of computer technology.

Computer Applications 8.2: EXPERT SYSTEMS

Prereading Activity

Discuss the following questions.

1. What is an expert? Give examples of people you know who are experts in their fields.

2. Read the following statements about computers. Write whether you *agree* or *disagree* in the blank space before each statement. Base your answers on your own opinions. Then compare and discuss your responses with those of your classmates.

     a. _____ Computers can help people learn.

     b. _____ Computers have the ability to learn.

     c. _____ Computers function more effectively and efficiently than human beings.

     d. _____ It is impossible to design and build a computer that can think like a human being.

     e. _____ Computers can help managers in the decision-making process.

     f. _____ The decision of a human being is always better than a decision recommended by an expert system.

Vocabulary

Below is a list of terms that you will find in the text. As you read "Expert Systems," see if you understand each term. Use this as a working list and add other terms that you do not know.

NOUNS	VERBS	ADJECTIVES	OTHERS
clarification	run	accessible	largely
assumption	respond	static	prior to
labor cost	challenge	repetitive	_____
feedback	apply	applicable	_____
knowledge base	translate	effective	_____
setting	interview	unique	
concept	recommend	_____	
symbol	perform	_____	
consistency	enhance		
productivity	_____		
_____	_____		
_____			
_____			

EXPERT SYSTEMS

Expert systems are the major business application of artificial intelligence (AI). In the broad view, AI is the ability of the computer to simulate the human thought process. Prior to the development of the first expert systems in 1984, research on AI had taken place largely in university and corporate research labs. Early AI pro-
5 grams proved costly and very time-consuming to develop and required special programming languages. These AI applications also required the most powerful and expensive computer systems. The more recent developments in AI-based expert systems, which are able to run on personal computers, have allowed AI applications to become more affordable and accessible to a variety of businesses.

10 An expert system is also known as a knowledge-based system. It differs from a database, where there is a static relationship between the data elements; for example, product name and cost fields have a fixed relationship with the inventory record. An expert system is interactive, responding to questions, asking for clarification, and modifying the knowledge base as it gets user feedback. Acting as a
15 consultant, the expert system aids in the decision-making process. At many levels of the organization, expert systems help employees improve their decision-making process by challenging common assumptions and providing an alternate method of analysis.

Other advantages of expert systems include:

20 • *availability*—An expert system is available for use 24 hours a day. It does not have to rest, nor can it decide to change jobs as a human expert can. The expert system can be accessed by anyone in the organization. Copies of the system can be made and distributed to a number of users.

• *cost*—The cost of developing an expert system has been decreasing. Use
25 of such a system saves labor costs in a repetitive decision-making environment.

• *memory*—An expert system has a greater range of knowledge than any one human expert. It also "learns" from user feedback and adds to its knowledge base. When the expert system is next needed, it provides more applic-
30 able information to the user and is, therefore, more effective with use.

Disadvantages of expert systems include the inability to apply a common-sense approach to a unique situation due to reliance upon rules. Expert systems currently operate in restricted settings. Even with recent developments, they must still translate concepts into symbols before processing this information.
35 To develop a computer-based expert system, knowledge engineers first interview human experts about their areas of expertise, for instance, distribution routes. Then these engineers and programmers translate their human knowledge about various transportation strategies and costs into a knowledge base. After the knowledge base is ready, the user asks the expert system for a recom-
40 mended distribution route for 20 large boxes of aircraft parts from Seattle to Tokyo. Next the expert system leads the user through a series of questions regarding weight and specific content of the shipment. Finally, the expert system recommends transporting the boxes by ship and estimates the cost.

The people involved in the development of an expert system are:

45

When matching the decisions made by expert systems against real human experts, the expert systems generally perform well. As expert systems are better planned, implemented, and managed, the reliability of their recommendations will continue to improve. Applying expert systems technology to business can improve accuracy and consistency, increase speed and productivity, reduce costs, and enhance the decision-making environment.

50

Comprehension

A. Answer the following questions about expert systems. Questions with asterisks (*) cannot be answered directly from the text.

★★

1. What is artificial intelligence (AI)? What is the primary business use of AI? *What other AI applications are you familiar with?
2. When were the first expert systems developed?
3. What were three disadvantages of the early AI programs?

★★★

4. *Why are expert systems less costly than the early AI programs?
5. What is the difference between a database and an expert system?
6. What are some advantages and disadvantages of applying expert system technology?
7. How is a computer-based expert system developed?
8. What is the knowledge engineer's job? What other people help develop an expert system?
9. How can the reliability of an expert system be improved?
10. *If you were the general manager of a small manufacturing business, how could you use an expert system?

★★ B. Determine which of the following statements are *true* and which are *false*. Then put T and F in the blanks. Rewrite false statements to make them true.

1. _*F*_ The relationship between the data elements is static in an expert system.

2. _____ An expert system works well in a repetitive decision-making environment.

3. _____ The costs of AI programs have been increasing.

4. _____ Only a manager can access and make use of an expert system.

5. _____ Human experts are an integral part of the development of expert systems.

Vocabulary Exercises

★★ A. Substitute appropriate terms for the italicized words or phrases in the sentences below.

interviewed	challenge	largely	✔ symbols	respond
accessible	repetitive	run	setting	assumptions

1. Knowledge engineers translate problem concepts into *signs* and rules. *symbols*

2. The computer revolution has *mainly* taken place in the late twentieth century. _____

3. Computerization can streamline *recurring* business operations. _____

4. Computer technology has enhanced the work *environment* of many offices. _____

5. An interactive computer program is one that can *reply* to user questions. _____

6. In developing an expert system for an insurance company, knowledge engineers *questioned* human experts. _____

7. Expert systems are now able to *work* on personal computers. _____

8. Information stored in an expert system is *easily obtained* when needed. _____

★★★ B. Discuss the following questions with a partner. In giving your answers, try to use the italicized words.

1. What are some *unique* characteristics of human beings?
2. Is *consistency* in expert system recommendations important? Why or why not?
3. How do you think the *knowledge base* of an expert system compares to the human brain?
4. Are computers *applicable* to any of your daily activities? Which ones?
5. What are factors that affect the *productivity* of a business?

★★★ C. Fill in the blanks with the most appropriate terms from the list.

labor costs	✔ applies	unique	recommends	consistency
challenges	enhanced	static	productivity	effective

An international rent-a-car company _____*applies*_____ expert system technology for setting car rental prices. The expert system _____ prices for different kinds of cars in a variety of cities. Since these prices are not _____, they need to be evaluated and revised constantly. In using an expert system to set rental prices, the rent-a-car company has decreased its _____, improved _____ and _____, and _____ the overall car pricing aspect of the business vis-à-vis competitors. The rent-a-car company has found the expert system very _____.

Text Analysis

Look at the reading to answer these questions.

⭐ 1. What does each of the following refer to?

LINES	WORDS	REFERENTS
10	it	_____
16	their	_____
28	its	_____
33	they	_____

2. In lines 11–12 and 36, connectives introduce examples. What are these connectives and examples?

CONNECTIVES   EXAMPLES

a. _____   _____

b. _____   _____

3. In lines 13–14, the ways in which an expert system is interactive are explained using three examples. What are these examples?

a. _____

b. _____

c. _____

⭐⭐⭐ 4. The reading details advantages and disadvantages of applying expert systems in the decision-making process. What are some of these advantages and disadvantages?

ADVANTAGES   DISADVANTAGES

a. _____   a. _____

b. *availability*   b. _____

c. _____   c. *translate concepts into symbols*

d. _____

5. Connective or key words and phrases are used to introduce each of the four steps in developing an expert system. What are these connectives and steps?

CONNECTIVES/PHRASES   STEPS

a. _____   a. _____

b. *then* _____   b. _____

c. _____   c. _____

d. _____   d. _____

e. _____   e. *The expert system recommends transporting the boxes by ship and estimates the cost.*

Writing

★★★   Your supervisor has asked you to find out about the benefits of **using expert systems**. You have just finished your research. Write a memo to **your supervisor summarizing** the advantages of applying expert system technology **in a business** environment. (For memo format, see "Management," page 119.)

Information Transfer

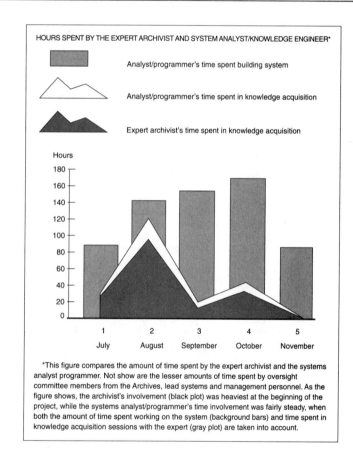

HOURS SPENT BY THE EXPERT ARCHIVIST AND SYSTEM ANALYST/KNOWLEDGE ENGINEER*

Analyst/programmer's time spent building system

Analyst/programmer's time spent in knowledge acquisition

Expert archivist's time spent in knowledge acquisition

*This figure compares the amount of time spent by the expert archivist and the systems analyst programmer. Not show are the lesser amounts of time spent by oversight committee members from the Archives, lead systems and management personnel. As the figure shows, the archivist's involvement (black plot) was heaviest at the beginning of the project, while the systems analyst/programmer's time involvement was fairly steady, when both the amount of time spent working on the system (background bars) and time spent in knowledge acquisition sessions with the expert (gray plot) are taken into account.

Barry Silverman, *Expert Systems for Business*, © 1987, by Addison-Wesley Publishing Company, Inc. Reprinted with permission of the publisher.

Figure 2

★★   A. Scan Figure 2 to answer these questions.

1. What's another term used for knowledge engineer?

_____

2. During which month did the expert archivist spend the most time?

_____ The least time? _____

3. Which month did both analyst/programmer and expert archivist spend the least time on knowledge acquisition? _____

4. How many hours did the analyst/programmer spend building the system in September? _____ In July? _____

5. In which month did the time spent building the system double from the time spent in November? _____

★★★   **B. Refer to Figure 2 to answer these questions.**

1. Approximately how many hours over a five-month period did the systems analyst/knowledge engineer spend building the system? _____

2. Which month shows the least amount of time spent in all three categories?

_____

3. What are the two tasks that the analyst/programmer works on? _____ Why do you think the analyst/programmer's time is divided into these two categories? _____

4. Approximately how many hours were spent developing the expert system from July through November? _____

5. Which of the three tasks took the most time? _____ Why? _____

Additional Activities

1. Visit a store that sells computer software. Choose a program that interests you, read about it, and try it out at the store. Then write a summary of its uses.
2. Interview a business executive to find out how much management time goes into information analysis and decision making. Consider whether that business would benefit from an expert system; then write a recommendation as if you were a management consultant.
3. Discuss the areas of your own life that could be helped by an expert system. How would it help?

Computer Applications 8.3: SOLVING A "STOCK OUT" PROBLEM

Warm-up

1. Look at the organizational chart for Monarch Retail Stores. It shows how the key management positions are structured.

Monarch Retail Stores

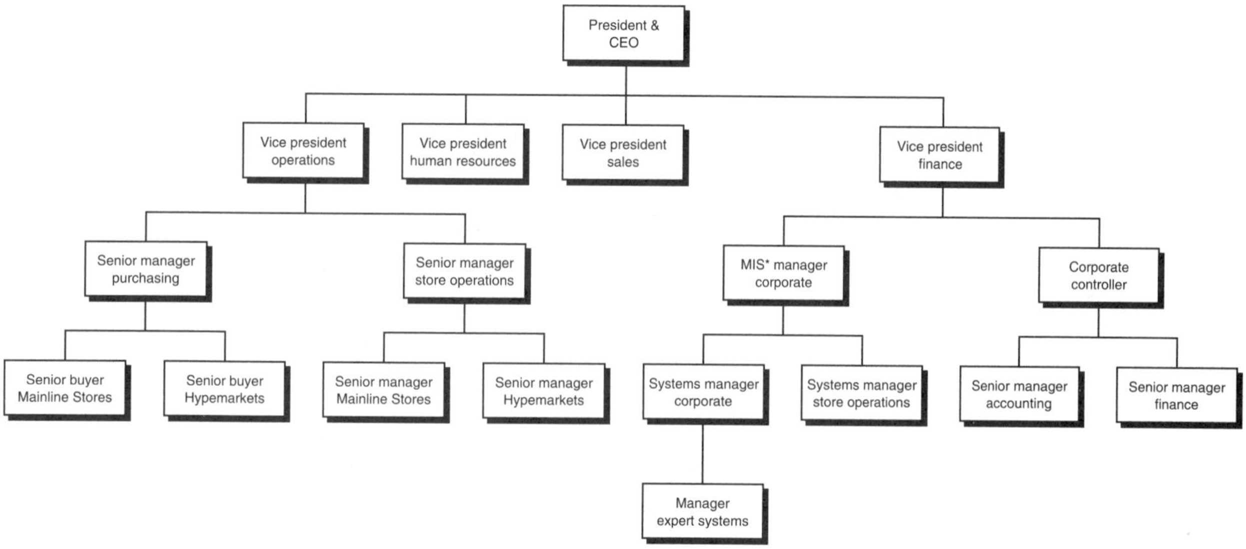

*MIS = Management Information Systems

Figure 3

2. How many vice presidents does Monarch Retail Stores have? _____

What is the highest position within this organization? Is this position held by one person? What does CEO mean? _____

What is the lowest level position shown here? _____

Who does the senior manager for Mainline stores report to? _____

What two positions are directly under the vice president for finance?

_____

3. Monarch Retail Stores has an Executive Committee. Who do you think sits on this committee? _____

_____

4. Why are organizational charts used to show the structure of companies?

_____

_____

Preparation

Read and discuss the following information about Monarch Retail Stores.

BACKGROUND

Monarch Retail Stores has been in business since 1908. Monarch currently operates 102 retail stores in 45 cities. These stores are of two types—the Mainline stores and the Hypermarkets. The Mainline stores are the older style Monarch stores. They sell groceries and a small variety of other items. These stores cater to individual neighborhood preferences. Mainline stores account for 65 percent of all sales. These stores serve the traditional Monarch customer.

The 16 Hypermarket stores are five to seven times larger than Mainline stores. These stores were started in the early 1980s to serve as regional shopping centers in rapidly growing areas. Hypermarkets carry groceries, clothing, electronic equipment, housewares, auto supplies, and many categories of other items.

Hypermarket sales are increasing 20 to 30 percent per year, whereas Mainline stores increase 3 to 5 percent per year. It is expected that by the end of the next fiscal year Hypermarket sales will be 50 percent of all Monarch stores sales. Overall, Monarch is viewed by customers and retail industry observers as a growing and innovative company that emphasizes customer satisfaction, quality products, and aggressive pricing.

Integrated Task

1. Read and discuss the problem below.

MONARCH'S "STOCK OUT"* PROBLEM

Mainline and Hypermarket stores have a stock out problem because their buyers cannot keep up with sales growth. There are simply too many items and too much sales volume to individually place orders for all items. Frequently, the distribution warehouses do not have enough stock on hand to fill store managers' daily requests for restock items. Therefore, distribution warehouse personnel give some of the items to each store but not enough for customer demand. Stores must issue rainchecks to customers when the item runs out. This is a time-consuming procedure for cashiers, slows down the checkout process for all customers, and causes a loss of sales, as few customers use the rainchecks at a later date. The customers are also unhappy about not being able to buy the desired item.

---

* items not available in sufficient quantity for customers to purchase

2. You are going to participate in a business simulation. Read the following information about the three different groups of participants.

   - The Executive Committee is composed of five members—the president and CEO, and the four vice presidents.
   - The MIS Expert Systems Task Force is made up of half of the remaining participants.
   - The Operations group is composed of the other half of the participants.

   Initially, managers representing the vice president of operations served on the MIS Expert System Task Force. However, when the Task Force decided to recommend a completely new method for purchasing, these members stopped actively participating. The vice president of operations requested that a group be formed from the purchasing and store operations units to prepare an alternative set of recommendations for the Executive Committee to consider. This task force is known as the Operations Group.

3. Divide into the three groups described above. The Executive Committee has requested that the MIS Expert Systems Task Force and the Operations Group make short presentations to them, complete with handouts and charts, in order to resolve the stock out problem. Directions for all three groups are in Appendix B, on page 181. Following the presentations, the Executive Committee will choose an approach.

Follow-up

1. Prepare a written report including charts to accompany your recommendation to the Executive Committee. If you are a member of the Executive Committee, write a memo justifying which approach to the stock out problem you have selected.
2. Videotape the presentations of the MIS Expert Systems Task Force and the Operations Group and the response of the Executive Committee.
3. Visit a local business and interview key personnel regarding their inventory and ordering systems. Find out how they avoid the stock out problem. Then make an oral presentation or written report based on your interview.
4. Fill in the organizational chart below either for the business you visited in #3 or for another organization with which you are familiar. Add and/or delete boxes as necessary. Then discuss your chart with your classmates.

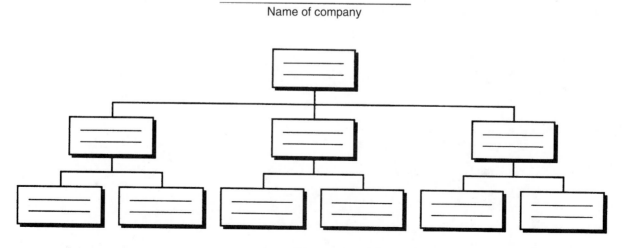

Name of company

Figure 4

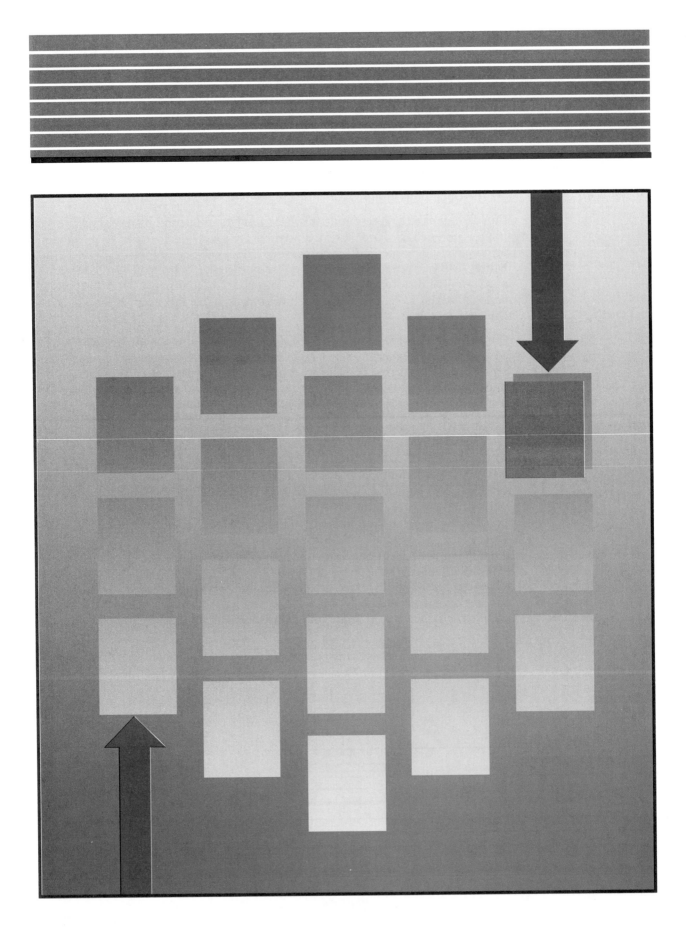

Appendices

A. Management 6.3: Looking at Leadership Styles

B. Computer Applications 8.3: Solving a "Stock Out" Problem

C. One Man's Model for Case Analysis

D. Case Studies

Appendix A

Instructions to the Three Leaders

Note: You should be away from the classroom when you are reading and discussing this. When you are ready, join the class and begin your leadership roles.

1. Each of you will assume the role of one of the three types of leaders: autocratic, participative, or laissez-faire. Please review the definitions on pages 130–131, and then decide who will assume each leadership style.
2. In the classroom, three groups of students are waiting for you. One of you will go to each group and lead them for ten minutes, being careful to demonstrate the leadership style you have chosen. After about ten minutes, you will go to the next group. Continue in the same role. After ten minutes with the second group, you will move on to the third group. Do *not* reveal your leadership style to the groups.
3. Your job, which will be the same for each group you meet with, is to lead your group to complete the following task in about ten minutes.

   Design the reception room of a large corporation. Draw it on paper, including the size and shape of the room, lighting, and types of furniture and location (including the reception desk).

Appendix B

Computer Applications 8.3: SOLVING A "STOCK OUT" PROBLEM

Instructions to the Three Groups

1. Executive Committee

The president and CEO is very concerned about the recent stock out occurrences. This problem has inconvenienced customers and negatively affected sales. The vice presidents of sales and finance are known to favor the Task Force's recommendations, though reliability of the expert system approach is a major issue with the vice president of sales. The vice president of operations favors the work of the Operations Group. The vice president of human resources has not shown any preference. The president and CEO insists that, following the presentations, a decision be made based on feasibility, cost, and reliability of the proposed solution.

The Executive Committee may want to use the form below to aid in the decision-making process.

MONARCH RETAIL STORES' STOCK OUT PROBLEM		
ALTERNATIVES	**ADVANTAGES**	**DISADVANTAGES**
1. Operations Group proposal		
2. MIS Expert Systems Task Force proposal		
Final recommendation		

2. MIS Expert Systems Task Force

Background

Your MIS Task Force is proposing that an expert system be set up to calculate the daily store inventory requirements for all items. This system would track sales history, promotional programs, and inventory item sales trends for each item sold by Monarch. This data would be sorted by Mainline and Hypermarket stores. The Task Force's plan calls for each store to report sales, transmitted hourly from electronic cash registers tied into the computer system. The expert system would automatically compute the number of required replacement items, check the stock on hand in the distribution warehouses, determine all other stores' requirements for the same item, and then if required, place an order electronically with a supplier.

The buyers working with store management would be responsible for selecting suppliers, determining new items to be stocked, and approving electronic orders greater than a certain monetary amount. This plan is projected to require a large cost initially for equipment purchases and program development. Once implemented, the expert system would operate more efficiently than the current buyer-directed system.

Presentation

Your presentation will focus on the following key strengths of the expert-based system:

- Ability to grow as sales volume and store numbers increase
- Better use of buyers' skills
- More cost-effective use of stores' and buyers' time
- Greater customer satisfaction and convenience
- Ability to analyze and respond quickly to large amounts of data

Your task force understands that there will be tough questions about:

- Feasibility of expert systems in general and particularly about the ability to do this specific task
- Initial start-up costs, which will be several million U.S. dollars
- Ability to be flexible enough to respond to real customer demand without causing large overstocks of unwanted items in the distribution warehouses
- Loss of control by store management and buyers over the reordering process
- Loss of creativity in response to problems or demands

With the support of the vice presidents of sales and finance, both of whom are key members of the Executive Committee, you are confident that your recommendations will be approved. This is an ambitious project; therefore, your operating motto has been "Promise only what can be delivered."

3. Operations Group

Background

Your Operations Group agrees that the current number of buyers cannot keep up with the growth in inventory items and sales volume. The Hypermarket stores' success has caused the number of inventory items to increase five-fold in ten years. Double-digit sales increases during the past seven years have nearly tripled total annual sales. Yet the number of persons responsible for purchasing has increased only 40 percent. The increased use of computer technology has made the system more efficient, but the current buyer staff is overwhelmed by the level of activity.

Your plan calls for increasing the total number of buyers by 50 percent. This would increase the number of buyers for the Mainline stores by 30 percent and the Hypermarket stores by 100 percent.

Presentation

Your presentation will focus on the following strengths of expanding the current system:

- Current system reliable until understaffing resulted in current stock out problem
- Moderate start-up costs
- Flexibility to adapt to changing consumer buying habits
- Traditional close communications and involvement between buyers and store management, who control the purchasing system

The areas where you feel most vulnerable to questions are as follows:

- Continual need to hire more buyers to keep pace with increasing sales volume and inventory item growth
- Long-term personnel costs because of the need to increase the number of buyers
- Lack of use of new, innovative technological tools

The vice president of operations is solidly behind these recommendations, yet the vice president of sales needs to be convinced. You will stress reliability to the vice president of sales. Your group believes that the vice president for human resources sees the increase in buying staff as being good for the human resources area. The president and CEO wants a solution as soon as possible. Your Operations Group believes that the set of recommendations to the Executive Committee can be fully implemented one year before the new expert system. Your group's motto is "proven reliability and proven results."

Appendix C

Step 1.   *What are the facts?*

This step involves relisting the major facts presented by the case. The purpose is to *systematically* summarize the facts, and thereby:

a. test for unclarities
b. develop an organized sense of the whole
c. discover differences in reading (among the group)

Note: Someone's opinion is not a fact, but an important fact may be that someone holds such and such an opinion.

Step 2.   *What can one infer from the facts?*

We can make many kinds of inferences from the facts, including inferences about:

a. people's attitudes
b. internal relations
c. relative power and influence
d. the requirements of the job (e.g., high technical skills)
e. relevant criteria for success (e.g., delivery more important than cost)

All such inferences are speculative and may often be only tentative or contradictory (e.g., we could infer from his statement that he is ignorant of the prior event or that he has knowledge of the prior event and is playing dumb).

Such inferences grow out of one's knowledge and theory of human behavior, organizations, and economics. They contribute hypotheses or probability statements. Managers must often make decisions and initiate action on the basis of just such judgments of what is probably the true situation. Thus, these inferences may be a basis for deciding on a course of action later on.

Step 2A.   *What is going on here?*

An alternative to Step 2 is to analyze what is going on here and why. This is particularly useful in terms of human behavior.

Analyze why someone is angry; why the company is under such time pressure, why there is so little contact between departments, and so forth.

Step 3.   *What problems exist, and why?*

The obvious problem or the problem stated by the characters in the case is often not a real problem or not the most basic problem.

---

*This outline was developed by R.D. Willits. It appears in the teacher's manual to accompany *Effective Behavior in Organizations*, revised edition, by Allan Cohen, Stephen Fink, Herman Gadon, and Robin Willits. 1980, pp. 113–14.

The second part of this step is to attempt to analyze why the problems exist. This can often lead to the recognition of more basic problems. The direct problem of insufficient output, when analyzed, might be due to a lack of coordination between two departments, thus suggesting that poor departmental relations is a more basic problem.

Also note the importance of seeking *multiple* causes for problems and not just a single cause.

Step 3A. *What additional information do I need to analyze this case adequately?*

Often we can get needed additional data from common references. Sometimes a decision may have to be made without such data but a thorough analysis at least includes recognizing what one would do in a real situation and explicitly stating any assumptions you are making about such data.

Step 4. *What are some possible solutions to the problems?*

It is easy to settle for one or two solutions. I'd suggest adopting a brain-storming approach, which focuses on thinking up a number of possibilities, with little concern if some are "far out." After focusing on numbers then focus on evaluating them, but first seek to be creative in thinking up a number of possible solutions.

Step 5. *What are the consequences of each alternative?*

I use the word *consequences* because it is neutral and includes positive as well as negative results.

Too often we settle for just one or the other, whereas most decisions have both costs and benefits. Identifying costs can also suggest ways to modify an alternative so as to reduce the costs. Seek more than one consequence. Too often we settle for only the one or two obvious consequences.

Step 6. *Decision and rationale for it:*

Here we come to the point of choice; which alternative do you choose, and *why*?

The "why" part is important. It involves putting together a systematic rationale for your choice and should often include anticipating and rebutting counterarguments. It should also explicitly state assumptions you are making.

Step 7. *What general ideas can be drawn from this case that might have application elsewhere?*

A case may often give emphasis to a theoretical concept, and this would be worth noting. It may add a further insight to the meaning or limitation of some theoretical concept. It may raise issues that warrant further thought. It may directly suggest new concepts or hypotheses worth applying in the future.

Note: Some cases do not really pose any problem, and therefore a decision is not appropriate. Steps 3–6 would be skipped. Such "analysis cases" are useful in sharpening skills of analysis and warrant considerable attention to steps 2, 2A, and 7. Step 2A sums up the focus one can usefully adopt with an analysis case.

Appendix D

The following nine cases from *Introduction to Modern Business* can be used as supplementary activities. They have been divided into five sections to correlate with the five units in this book.

I.1   **DEAD END**

Joe Dogeness received a business degree from a well-known university in 1986 and took a job with a large oil company. His career got off to a good start. By 1992, his salary was $38,000, and he was in charge of a five-person analysis team.

Joe was not happy with his career progress, however. Although his salary was satisfactory, his level of responsibility was only slightly greater than it had been during his first year or two with the company. He had been stuck in a staff job at the home office for six years and felt that he would like a change. He requested a transfer to a line-marketing job.

He was told that he was too valuable in his current job to be transferred. He was overpaid for a lower-level line position, and too inexperienced to be promoted to a middle- or upper-level line position.

1. What should Joe do?
2. Why has he gotten into this fix?

I.2   **I AM A SUCCESS!!**

Roberta Franklin got an M.B.A. in 1983 and went to work for a large New York consulting firm. Within a year, she was in charge of major projects throughout the country, which meant that she was away from home much of the time. Roberta assured her husband that this hectic pace would last only a few years and that she could then settle down to a more normal life.

In 1990, she went to work for a client firm as division personnel manager. But the job had been neglected for some years, and Roberta had to work long hours and weekends to straighten things out. By 1993 she had received two more promotions and was earning over $60,000. She was viewed as a real comer by top management.

Roberta paid a price. Her husband seldom saw her and finally asked for a divorce. Roberta has begun to question whether this is the kind of life she really wants. Much of the enjoyment she had had from her work is gone and she feels that her life is being wasted.

1. Roberta is very successful—what is the problem?
2. Where does she go from here?

Vernon A. Musselman and John H. Jackson, *Introduction to Modern Business*, ninth edition, © 1984, pp. 101, 242, 320–321, 377, 406–407, 492–493, 585, 610. Reprinted by permission of Prentice-Hall, Englewood Cliffs, New Jersey.

II.1   ADVERTISING A NEW SERVICE

Commercial banks are faced with increasing competition from savings and loans, credit unions, brokerage firms, and even retailers (such as Sears), which are all offering "bank-type" services. As a result of this increased competition, many banks are scrambling to offer new innovative services in order to retain their current customers and gain new accounts.

The local, home-owned bank, First National Bank of Laramie, Wyoming, wishes to compete head-to-head with the larger, multistate banks entering its market. In order to be competitive, it is introducing the 2001 account. This is a special account in which any deposit balance over $2,000 is swept into a money-market account that pays a high rate of interest. Consumers do not have to manage their money for the highest possible returns. The bank will perform this service for them.

In order to introduce this new service to the local community of 25,000 people, First National has budgeted $6,000 for three months of introductory advertising.

Which of the following media are most appropriate for the bank's campaign? Why?

a. National television
b. Magazines
c. Newspapers
d. Radio
e. Direct mail (statement stuffers)

Is there a role for any of the other elements of the promotional blend (personal selling, sales promotion, publicity) in introducing this service? Why, or why not?

II.2   IMPORT GOODS TO BROADEN SALES?

The Lacy Ceramics Company, located in Ohio, makes wholesale, low-price dishes. It sells its product to so-called dishbarns and to discount stores throughout middle America. Last year's sales were $20 million.

The company would like to expand by handling a line of low-priced imported china. The firm's marketing manager is convinced that there is a market for such a line. The company vice president suggested that goods be bought from Taiwan. The company treasurer thinks it would be better to buy from English firms.

The company purchasing agent thinks that agents in New York who buy foreign goods should be used. The sales manager wants to send someone to England and Asia on a scouting mission. (In fact, he hopes to make the trip himself.) The company president's only input is that the firm should start on a small scale.

1. How can the management learn about Taiwanese and English china?
2. What information should the management obtain in order to make a preliminary decision in this situation?
3. Assuming a decision is made to take on a line of imported china, what are some things that must be decided?

III.1   SHOULD THE DECKER COMPANY EXPAND?

The Decker Appliance Company, which produces a line of home appliances, has an excellent reputation for high-quality merchandise. The company sells its appliances to two chain stores under separate private-label brands. The two chains buy virtually the entire output of Decker products each year. Both companies have contracts that will expire in another ten months. Each chain has informed the Decker management that it would like to sign a new three-year contract that would result in a substantial increase in the company's annual production. To do this, the company would have to expand its plant by adding new and more modern equipment.

Tentative estimates indicate that a proposed production expansion would involve the need for new financing amounting to $1 million.

The Decker Company, a close corporation owned by four members of the Decker family, is capitalized at $5 million, with 100,000 shares of common stock outstanding, with a par value of $50. The company recently retired its preferred stock. There are no bonds. Its credit is the highest rating available, according to Dun & Bradstreet.

The stock is sold over the counter, but transactions seldom occur, since there are only about 500 shares held outside the Decker family. The last quoted price was $40 per share. The dividend last year was $2.80 per share, with annual earnings of $500,000. As an investment, the stock yields 7 percent.

At a meeting of the stockholders and the board of directors, various proposals were discussed. One plan consisted of financing the expansion from earnings and leasing. A second plan was to amend the charter and increase the number of shares of authorized common stock from 100,000 to 200,000. The company would then sell 25,000 shares of common at $40 per share. This would produce $1 million.

1. If you were a stockholder of the Decker Company, how would you feel about expanding the plant's production?
2. Which plan for financing the expansion do you prefer?
3. What risks do you see in increasing production?

III.2 ALAMO PUMP CORPORATION HAS GROWING PAINS

The Alamo Pump Corporation was organized in 1969 to manufacture water pumps for irrigation systems and industrial plants. The corporation owns three important patents related to water and steam valves. Its products are sold mainly through farm-implement dealers. Alamo's general office is in San Antonio, Texas. Its stock is locally owned.

Last year the corporation earned 5 percent on sales of $1 million and paid a dividend of 50 cents per quarter on 12,000 shares of common stock. During peak production periods, usually during the summer months, Alamo often experiences a shortage of working capital, which requires one or more short-term bank loans. However, the new treasurer, a stockholder, is critical of this practice of borrowing. He contends that the corporation should plan to avoid peak production periods. Following is a recent simplified balance sheet:

Alamo Pump Corporation

ASSETS		LIABILITIES	
Cash	$ 50,000	Notes payable	$ 10,000
Accounts receivable	800,000	Accounts payable	300,000
Merchandise inventory	70,000	Common stock (20,000 shares,	
Machinery	100,000	$3 per share per value)	60,000
Land and buildings	100,000	Surplus	750,000
Total assets	$1,120,000	Total liabilities and capital	$1,120,000

1. Do you agree with Alamo's treasurer?
2. What is Alamo's main problem, and how can it be solved?
3. What other sources of short-term credit can you suggest?

IV.1 PROBLEMS IN LOGISTICS

The Hartford Company operates a large public distribution center. During the past 12 months, a number of problems have become serious and resulted in reduced productivity. Area heads blame the workers and one another. The workers complain of a lack of coordination and inadequate supervision. They say that merchandise is unnecessarily being moved to new locations. They are not always sure to which "boss" they are accountable. The superintendent seems to have lost control over the area heads. Morale is low, and employees who have been with the company for many years are threatening to quit. The absentee owners, Elton and Everett Hartford, are considering several alternatives:

a. Appoint a committee of three area heads to make an analysis of the situation and recommend changes.
b. Hire a new superintendent and give him full control but keep the present area heads.
c. Employ an outside consultant.

What do you see as the strengths and/or weaknesses of each plan?

IV.2   WHAT'S WRONG WITH WESTERN TIRES, INC.?

Western Tires, Inc., with headquarters in Arizona, has been manufacturing automobile tires and fan belts for American-made automobiles. These products are marketed under the brand name of Wearwell through tire dealers and service stations as replacement parts. Carl and Lee Busch, brothers, established the company in 1923 and are still the principal shareholders. Carl owns 60 percent of the outstanding common stock, and Lee owns 20 percent. Six employees, including two of the company executives, own the remaining stock.

The company employs 225 men and women, with 23 working in the headquarters offices. Carl Busch is president, and Lee Busch is treasurer and is in charge of all accounting, including the payroll department. Lee has been trying to persuade Carl to install a computer. The plant superintendent has also submitted a request to use a computer for quality-control purposes in the plant. The president says this computer costs too much.

Union grievances are frequently filed, but few ever go to arbitration. Usually the president makes the final decision to make a settlement that the union is willing to accept. In general, the company's executives feel that the president lacks leadership qualities and does not know how to get along with others. He is also unwilling to delegate responsibility.

On several occasions, Lee has urged his brother to seek the directors' approval to appoint an executive vice-president. Lee feels that this executive could take over some of the duties now performed by the president.

Last month, the president was ill for 24 days because of a stroke. Carl's physician has advised him that he must reduce his workload and delegate more authority to others. During Carl's illness, the company lost a large contract with a fleet owner for 500 replacement tires. When this was discovered, two directors asked the president for an explanation. They wanted to know why he had not authorized his brother, Lee, to negotiate this pending contract.

1. What is wrong with the company organization?
2. What action would you take to solve the company's problems if you were in charge?

V.1   OPTIMIZE COMPUTER RESOURCES

Two years ago, Uintah Energy Company, a medium-sized gas and oil exploration company, purchased a minicomputer system. The computer can operate in both batch processing and on-line real-time modes. At the time of purchase, the company's bookkeeper, a high school graduate, was sent to a one-week computer training school. She is now manager of the computer department, which includes three other full-time data-processing employees. Since the time of purchase, the manager has used the computer to automate payroll, accounts receivable, accounts payable, the general ledger, and preparation of financial statements.

The president of Uintah wants the data-processing manager to expand the use of the computer into decision-making jobs, but she is uncertain if such applications should be automated. She feels that the company is deriving sufficient dollar benefits from the jobs currently automated.

1. Do you agree with the president?
2. Is Uintah optimizing the computer resource?
3. What types of benefits do you feel the company is receiving from its automated applications?
4. What types of benefits should it be receiving?
5. Assuming that the company expands its computer usage into decision-making jobs, do you feel that it will encounter any problems?

Glossary

The words listed in the Glossary come from the vocabulary lists preceding each reading. The terms are defined as they are used in the readings. Cross-references are provided for some business terms. If the vocabulary lists include adjective, adverb, noun, and verb forms of the same word, in some cases only the verb forms are listed and defined in the Glossary. The following abbreviations are used: n = noun; v = verb; adj = adjective; adv = adverb.

absolute advantage (n)   A theory of specialization that states a nation ought to specialize in the goods that it can produce more cheaply than its competitors or in the goods that no or few other nations are able to produce. (See also *comparative advantage.*)

access (v)   To get; to reach; to obtain.

accounting equation (n)   A fundamental concept representing the accounting position of a company: assets equal liabilities plus owners' (or stockholders') equity. (See also *owners' equity.*)

accuracy (n)   Correctness, freedom from errors.

achieve (v)   To accomplish; to successfully complete something.

acquire (v)   To obtain; to gain possession of.

adequately (adv)   Sufficiently; satisfactorily.

adopt (v)   To take up; to act in accordance with.

advancement (n)   Upward movement; promotion.

advantageous (adj)   Beneficial; profitable.

advise (v)   To suggest or recommend; to offer advice or counsel.

affect (v)   To bring about a change; to influence.

affordable (adj)   Able to be bought fairly reasonably.

agency (n)   A type of organization that usually acts for others and that provides a service.

allocate (v)   To set aside or distribute for a specific purpose.

allow (v)   To permit something to happen or exist.

alter (v)   To modify; to change by degree.

alternative (n)   A choice or option; in decision-making, a potential solution to a problem.

analytic (adj)   Pertaining to careful study of something to determine its nature.

appeal to (v)   To be of interest or to be attractive.

applicable (adj)   Capable of being used; appropriate; relevant.

application (n)   The use of a theory or technique to achieve a desired outcome.

apply (v)   To adapt or use for a special purpose.

appreciation of (n)   Awareness or perception of.

aptitude (n)   A natural or acquired capability to learn and understand quickly; a talent for something.

arrangement (n)   Settlement; agreement (e.g., to negotiate a financial *arrangement* with a bank).

assemble (v)   To put together, until complete, the various components of a larger unit.

asset (n)   Anything of value that a person or business owns that can be given a monetary value (e.g., property, cash, equipment).

assume (v)   To take upon oneself; to undertake the responsibility for.

assumption (n)   A statement accepted or supposed true without proof or demonstration.

attain (v)   To achieve; to successfully complete something.

attempt (v)   To try; to make an effort.

authority (n)   The right and power to determine, act, or influence.

available (adj)   Obtainable; easy to gain access to.

aware (adj)   Conscious of; understanding what is happening.

background (n)   A person's experience, training, and education.

base (n)   (1) A primary location for an organization's activities. (2) The foundation upon which all else is built.

blend (v)   To mix; to intermingle.

bond (n)   A certificate of indebtedness issued by a corporation for a specific period of time (maturity date) that includes the initial amount received (principal)   plus periodic payments made by the company (interest) to the investor.

borrow (v)   To solicit and obtain funds (money) for a specified period with a promise to repay, secured by assets.

capable (adj)   Having the ability or skill for.

capacity (n)   The maximum amount that can be held or manipulated at one time—for example, in referring to computers, the size and sophistication of the CPU (central processing unit); the shortest amount of time the CPU requires to process multiple transactions.

capital (n)   The money needed to start and continue operating a business. Also, the total funds invested in a firm, or net worth (the excess of assets over liabilities).

career (n)   The chosen work of one's life.

categorize (v)   To classify; to put into classes.

challenge (v)   To take exception to; to dispute or question.

channel of distribution (n)   The path goods take when moving—first from the manufacturer and ultimately to the customer. (See also *retailer* and *wholesaler*.)

charge (v)   To set as a price; to demand payment for goods or services.

charge account (n)   A credit agreement whereby a customer or client receives goods or services prior to making payment.

chip (n)   An integrated circuit used in computers and other high-tech products.

clarification (n)   The act of making something clearer by providing additional information.

classify (v)   To arrange or organize according to category.

clerical (adj)   Pertaining to routine business office tasks (e.g., keeping records and accounts, filing, and typing).

combination (n)   Union; the state of being brought together (e.g., the marketing mix is a *combination* of the four P's).

communicate (v)   To make known; to impart.

comparative advantage (n)   A theory of specialization that states a nation ought to concentrate on the products that it can produce most efficiently and profitably. (See also *absolute advantage*.)

competitor (n) A rival, or opponent, who is trying to attract the same customer or to work in the same market.

complex (adj) Complicated; involved.

component (n) A part or element that (in conjunction with additional parts or elements) forms a larger, more complex unit—usually mechanical or electrical.

computer language (n) The technical codes that must be used to write a computer program. Languages can be divided into two classes: (1) machine codes, which are directly understood by the computer, and (2) autocodes, such as FORTRAN and COBOL. Autocodes are easier to use but they must be converted into machine codes by a special program known as a compiler. (See also *computer program*.)

computer program (n) A detailed set of instructions that tells the computer what to do, how to do it, and the proper sequence of steps to follow to solve a problem or perform an action.

concept (n) A general idea or understanding, especially one derived from specific instances or occurrences.

condition (n) The existing circumstance.

consequently (adv) Therefore; as a result.

consideration (n) A factor to be examined carefully before making a decision or forming a judgment.

consistency (n) Regularity of action; compatibility or agreement among successive acts, ideas, or events.

conversion (n) The change or transformation of one substance, alone or in conjunction with other materials, into a substance having a different appearance or different properties than the original product.

corporation (n) A type of business organization, formed by an association of stockholders, that has a special type of legal charter.

correct (adj) Accurate; proper.

create (v) To bring about; to cause to happen.

creative (adj) Artistic, skilled, talented.

creativity (n) Imagination; the ability to come up with new ideas.

credit extension (n) A line of short-term financing provided to a retailer by either a distributor or a manufacturer in return for the sale of a given product(s).

current (adj) In accounting, *current* assets are things of value (owned by a company or an individual) that can easily be changed into cash; *current* liabilities are debts (owed by a company or an individual) that must be repaid within one year.

currently (adv) Now; at this time.

data (n) The raw material from which information is derived (e.g., computerized information systems process *data* into user-required information).

data processing (n) A rather all-encompassing term relating to the computerized collection, communication, analysis, and summarization of data.

deadline (n) A time limit for completing something.

decision-making (n) The process of choosing among alternative courses of action in order to achieve an objective.

demand (n) Need; requests for use (e.g., customer *demand* for a product).

depend on (v) To rely on for help or support.

describe (v) To present with words a mental image, an impression, or something that has happened.

detail (v) To carefully provide information, item by item, with concern for accuracy.

determine (v) To establish conclusively after observation or analysis.

development (n)   A process of growth or expansion in which something increases in both size and complexity.

direct (v)   (1) To focus attention, activity, or resources toward an objective; to aim. (2) The management function of guiding, teaching, and motivating employees in a manner consistent with the company's objectives.

direction (n)   Instruction and supervision of some action or operation.

dissatisfaction (n)   The state of not being pleased, especially when something desired has not been provided.

distribution (n)   The movement of finished products from the manufacturing location to the marketplace. One of the basic functional areas of business (the other two are production and sale of goods or services). The *distribution* stage of business consists of the marketing, merchandising, and transportation of manufactured goods or created services. (See also *production* and *sale*.)

domestic (adj)   Not foreign; of or pertaining to the "home country."

earn (v)   To acquire something because of one's behavior (e.g., to *earn* wages or a salary).

effectively (adv)   Able to produce the intended or expected result; meeting the predetermined objective.

efficiently (adv)   Able to achieve the desired outcome using the fewest possible resources with the greatest amount of productivity.

electronic (adj)   Pertaining to systems based on the flow of electrons, which are particles having a negative charge.

element (n)   One of the parts of a whole.

enable (v)   To make possible; to provide an opportunity by supplying the means.

enhance (v)   To improve, increase, or make greater.

entitle (v)   To give one a right; to allow or allot.

environmental (adj)   Pertaining to the surrounding conditions.

equal (v)   To have the same value as.

equipment (n)   Tangible unit or units, comprised of components that perform or assist business operations. In accounting usage, a major category of fixed assets.

essential (adj)   Necessary; indispensable.

establish (v)   To set up securely in a position or condition.

evaluate (v)   To deliberate; to fix a relative value between the desired outcome and the actual situation; to judge.

examine (v)   To look at in detail; to consider carefully.

exchange (n)   The process of trading or bartering one unit or set of goods or services for another unit or set.

exemplify (v)   To illustrate, or show, by the use of an example.

expand (v)   To increase the dimensions of; to enlarge in scope or complexity.

expect (v)   (1) To consider likely or probable. (2) To anticipate.

expectation (n)   Anticipation of a future action or state.

expenditure (n)   Resources that have already been committed or spent; an expense.

expenses (n)   The costs associated with performing a business activity (e.g., the money spent or disbursed for the wages of production workers).

experience (v)   To undergo; to encounter.

expertise (n)   Specialized knowledge or skill in a particular area.

export (v)   To ship to a nonlocal geographic location (usually to another country) finished products or raw materials for sale or trade. (See also *import*.)

express (v)   To indicate by words or symbols.

external (adj)   Relating to an outer part; not internal.

factor (n)   A contributing element or component in some process or outcome.

feasible (adj)   Possible to do or to undertake.

fee (n)   Charge for services provided (e.g., for public accountants).

feedback (n)   The return of a part of the output of any process or system to the input or user.

field (n)   (1) An area of interest or specialization. (2) *In the field:* in an operational phase of a marketing program in which the product is made available to the consumer.

finance (n)   An area of business that concentrates on securing and utilizing capital and other assets to start up, operate, or expand a company.

financial statement (n)   A summary of the major financial activities of an organization, issued on a periodic basis. Two types of *financial statements* are the balance sheet and the income statement.

fit (v)   To have the correct size and shape for.

fit into (v)   To agree with; to be appropriate for.

flexibility (n)   Adaptability; willingness to change (e.g., responsiveness to a changing business environment).

focus on (v)   To concentrate on; to center attention on.

force (v)   To make a person or thing do something.

foresee (v)   (1) To predict or anticipate. (2) To expect.

for instance For example.

the four P's (n)   The four main elements of marketing: product, price, placement, and promotion.

framework (n)   Any basic structure, arrangement, or outline.

frequently (adv)   Occurring often; not rarely.

fulfill (v)   To satisfy (e.g., to *fulfill* requirements).

function (n)   (1) Duty or occupational role (i.e., tasks for which a person is employed). (2) Use or activity (e.g., routine *functions* of computers).

fundamental (adj)   Essential; necessary (e.g., *fundamental* needs, such as a good salary and job security).

funds (n)   Financial resources available for a given purpose.

global (adj)   Of or pertaining to the entire world; universal.

goods (n)   Products that people either need or want to purchase or acquire. In economic usage, refers more specifically to tangible commodities or merchandise. (See also *services*.)

guarantee (v)   To assure; to promise.

guide (v)   To direct by showing the way.

habit (n)   A custom or usual practice.

handle (v)   To cope with, manage, or deal with a situation (e.g., to successfully *handle* a difficult business problem).

high-tech (adj)   High or advanced technology; used to describe something that applies recent technological advances.

hire (v)   To employ, usually resulting in the exchange of wages for labor.

ideal (adj)   Existing in the mind; often not practical or attainable.

identification (n)   Recognition; establishment of the identity of a person or thing.

implement (v)   To put into action (e.g., a plan or program).

import (v)   To bring in or receive finished goods or raw materials from another country. (See also *export*.)

incentive (n)   An encouragement or stimulus to produce additional effort.

independently (adv)   Not guided or directed by others.

in fact   Indeed; used to add emphasis to the preceding sentence(s).

influence (v)   To affect or change by indirect means.

informed (adj)   (1) Knowledgeable. (2) Based on prior knowledge of facts and information related to the situation.

initial (adj)   First; occurring at the very beginning.

innovative (adj)   (1) New or different. (2) Willing to introduce change and take a risk.

in order to   So that it is possible to.

insure (v)   To guarantee; to make sure.

integral (adj)   Essential or necessary for the whole.

integrate (v)   To make into a whole by bringing all parts together.

interaction (n)   The interpersonal relationship(s) that take place between two or more people.

interest payment (n)   An amount paid on a regular basis (in addition to the principal owed) for borrowing money.

internally (adj)   Relating to an inner part; not external.

interpersonal (adj)   Of or relating to relationships between people.

interpret (v)   To understand and explain the meaning or significance of something.

interview (n)   A face-to-face meeting arranged for the formal discussion of a specific subject between a reporter and a person from whom the reporter (interviewer) wants information.

inventory (n)   Stored amounts of raw materials, components, or finished products not yet used or sold. Generally considered as a current asset in accounting practice.

invest (v)   To spend or commit money (capital) or other resources (e.g., time) in order to gain some future advantage or to provide some benefit.

investment (n)   The expenditure of available capital resources in order to purchase either equipment or securities that will contribute to the achievement of the objectives of a business or an individual.

involve in (v)   To participate in; to take part in.

isolation (n)   Separation from others.

issue (v)   To offer or make available for sale or distribution (e.g., *issuing* stock).

knowledge base (n)   The foundation of a computer-based expert system that contains the specific information gathered from experts.

labor cost (n)   Of or associated with money paid to employees for work (salary or hourly wage and benefits)

lack (v)   To be without; to be deficient.

largely (adv)   Mainly; mostly.

last (v)   To continue to exist; to go on or endure.

lease (v)   To formally arrange, usually by contract, the transfer of use of property or machinery for a fixed period of time and for a specified amount of money.

liability (n)   A debt owed or an obligation incurred by an organization—for example, accounts payable, bonds, long-term notes. Usually separated into current and long-term categories for purposes of the accounting function.

likely (adv)   Probably; expected to happen.

likewise (adv)   Similarly; in the same way

limit (v)   To confine; to restrict to a lesser degree

list (v)   To record; to present in a particular arrangement.

long-term (adj)   Over a period of years; in finance, more than one year. (See also *short-term*.)

maintain (v)   To keep up efficiently; to not let something decline.

management (n)   A team of managers responsible for making sure—by planning, organizing, directing, and controlling—that an organization moves toward its objectives.

manager (n)   A person who has the skills or is in the position to oversee the functions of a business or organization.

manipulation (n)   Skillful handling or usage for a specific purpose (e.g., the CPU, or central processing unit, of a computer *manipulates* the input data into different configurations until the goals (output) of the user are achieved).

marketing (n)   The movement of goods and services from a business to its clients in order to satisfy customer demands as well as to achieve company objectives. (See also *the four P's.*)

marketing mix (n)   A combination of the four P's: product, price, placement, and promotion.

market research (n)   Studies that are used to determine the potential of a product (e.g., consumer preference).

match (v)   To put together so that a number of variables are suited for each other.

material (adj)   Referring to something physical rather than spiritual or intellectual.

meet (v)   To satisfy the requirements of.

mold (v)   To influence the formation of (e.g., to *mold* someone 's opinion).

monetary (adj)   Of or pertaining to money.

monitor (v)   To watch closely and systematically.

morale (n)   The mental condition of a group or individual; in business, demonstrated by the degree of enthusiasm or willingness to perform required tasks

motivate (v)   To move or stimulate into action; in a business context, to direct the behavior of workers toward company goals.

motivation (n)   That which causes or moves someone to take or follow a course of action, either self-determined or as suggested by others.

move on (v)   To continue to the next phase.

national (adj)   Relating to a whole country.

objective (n)   A statement derived from an organization's goals or statement of purpose that provides a target for a planned course of action.

obligation (n)   A legally binding debt that an individual or an organization has agreed to repay at some future date and that usually involves a penalty if it is not promptly repaid.

obtain (v)   To get; to succeed in acquiring.

offer (V)   To make available; to provide.

ongoing (adj)   Continuous; unending.

on the other hand But; however.

operate in (v)   To function in; to work in.

operation (n)   A process or series of acts performed to bring about a certain result.

option (n)   A choice available from a selection of alternatives.

organization (n)   Persons or groups working for a common purpose and whose tasks are often divided into specializations.

output (n)   (1) That which is produced or manufactured, usually in a specified period of time. (2) Relating to computer science, the data or information that is the end product of a computer program.

overall (adj)   Comprehensive; relating to a totality.

owe (v)   To be required to pay (e.g., to *owe* someone money).

own (v) To have or to possess (e.g., to *own* a car)

owners' equity (n) That which belongs to the owners or shareholders of a business after all liabilities have been subtracted from assets. (See also *accounting equation*.)

particular (adj) Specific; special.

party (n) A person or group of persons with a common interest.

payable (adj) Needing to be paid; due; in accounting, accounts *payable*. (See also *receivable*.)

payroll (n) (1) A listing of each employee in a company and the wages that are currently due to that person for the current pay period. (2) Also can refer to the total amount of wages paid to employees by a business (e.g., their *payroll* is very large).

perform (v) To do; to accomplish.

periodic (adj) Occurring at regular times or intervals.

personal (adj) Private; relating to an individual.

phase (n) One distinct stage of development in a sequence of activities or events.

physical (adj) Pertaining to a material or tangible thing; not spiritual or mental.

popularly (adv) Generally; widely accepted by people.

portable (adj) Something that is easily carried, for example, a *portable* computer.

position (n) A job within a company or organization.

potential (adj) Possible, but has not yet occurred or materialized.

practical (adj) Feasible; capable of being used or implemented.

prediction (n) A forecast of the outcome of an event before it occurs. The basis on which business planning and decision-making are founded.

present (v) To bring forth; to show.

price (v) To establish the cost for goods or services.

price leader (n) A company that controls a large enough share of a market to be a major factor in the pricing of the goods or services in that market.

print (v) To produce a copy on paper.

primary (adj) Chief; principal; main.

prior to Before.

procedure (n) The particular method by which something is processed.

process (v) To go through a series of steps or prescribed procedures. (n) A series of transactions or functions that bring about a particular result.

production (n) The functional area of business whereby services are created or raw materials are converted, through manufacturing, into finished products. One of the three basic functions of a business organization (the other two are distribution and sale of goods or services). The *production* phase of business encompasses product research and development, purchase of materials, and manufacturing. (See also *distribution* and *sale*.)

productivity (n) A measure of the efficiency of production; the amount of output of goods and services in a given period of time compared to the input of labor and capital.

profit (n) Theoretically, the monetary benefits earned by a business entity for risk-taking activities in the marketplace. Calculated in accounting terms as the difference between revenues and operations costs incurred by a business; most often used in conjunction with the capitalistic economic system. (See also *surplus*.)

promotion (n) Communication about a product or service initiated by the seller to influence potential buyers or clients (e.g., personal selling and advertising).

property (n)   Anything legally owned or possessed by a person or an organization.

proportional (adj)   Relating to a part or amount that is considered in relation to the whole.

purchase (v)   To buy; to obtain something in exchange for money.

quarterly (adv)   Relating to something that is done four times a year (e.g., a *quarterly* report).

quite (adv)   Rather; somewhat.

raw (adj)   Not processed; in the natural state (e.g., *raw* materials necessary for production).

reach (v)   To get to; to succeed in making contact.

reality (n)   (1) A perception of what is (subjective). (2) That which in fact exists (objective).

receivable (adj)   A business's accounts for goods or services already provided, for which payment is due and has not been received. (See also *payable*.)

recommend (v)   To call to the attention of someone else as reputable, worthy, or desirable; to endorse.

reflect (v)   To show; to indicate or manifest.

regardless of   In spite of; without concern for.

relate to (v)   To associate with; to connect to.

relationship (n)   An association or involvement between two or more individuals or entities.

relative (adj)   Comparative; considered in relation to something else; not absolute.

reliable (adj)   Able to be depended on.

rely on (v)   To depend on (e.g., to *rely on* computers to process and report data).

remain (v)   To stay or to be left after everything else is taken away.

repay (v)   To pay back (money).

repetitive (adj)   Characterized by saying, doing, or producing something again; recurring.

replace (v)   To provide a substitute for.

report (v)   To present an account and summation of an activity or the results of a project on a periodic or regular basis.

represent (v)   To express; to symbolize.

resource (n)   A supply of raw materials, goods, services, or expertise available for use when needed.

respond (v)   To reply; to answer.

restrict (v)   To limit.

retailer (n)   One who sells goods directly to customers. (See also *channel of distribution* and *wholesaler*.)

reveal (v)   To make known information that previously was not known.

revise (v)   To change something in the hope of making it better.

revolutionize (v)   To change dramatically.

rigorous (adj)   Difficult to fulfill or complete; strict; strenuous.

risk (n)   The possibility of (and uncertainty about) loss or damage. One of the factors affecting the decision-making process.

role (n)   Function.

rotate (v)   To systematically alternate (e.g., to *rotate* jobs or parts).

routine (adj)   Of or relating to habitual, ordinary procedures.

run (v)   To execute one or more computer programs.

salary (n)   A fixed amount of money earned by a person on a regular basis.

sale (n)   The exchange of ownership of products or services for money. Final phase of the three basic business functions—production and distribution being the first two phases. Whether products or services are sold by a producer, wholesaler, or retailer, there must be a buyer for the goods as well as a seller. (See also *distribution* and *production.*)

satisfy (v)   To please; to fulfill a desire, need, or expectation.

scarce (adj)   Something in short supply; not enough to meet demand.

schedule (v)   To make a plan that incorporates what is to be done and when it is to be done.

self-realization (n)   The fulfillment of one's potential capacities.

sequence (n)   A series of events occurring in succession; one following another in a random or predetermined order.

services (n)   Activities that a person or group performs for another person or organization; in business, usually involving a fee or monetary charge; in economic usage most often a nontangible commodity. (See also *goods.*)

setting (n)   The context or environment in which a situation occurs.

severe (adj)   Extreme; critical.

share (n)   A unit of ownership in a corporation, usually called stock, held by an individual or institution that gives entitlement to a portion of the growth and profits that the business produces. (See also *stock.*)

short-term (adj)   Reaching maturity in the not-too-distant future; in relation to financing, an arrangement in which money must be repaid in less than one year

similarly (adv)   Likewise; in the same way.

simulate (v)   To imitate; to replicate; to act like something else.

solely (adv)   Only; exclusively.

solve (v)   To answer or explain a given problem.

somewhat (adv)   To some degree; not completely.

source (n)   A place from which something can be gotten or received (e.g., capital is borrowed from internal and external *sources*).

specialize in (v)   To work exclusively in a specific area; to devote full-time attention to.

static (adj)   Unchanging; stationary.

stimulus (n)   An incentive; something that causes a response in thought, feeling, or action.

stock (n)   Investment made by the owners of a business (usually a corporation) that allows a share in growth and profitability as well as a vote in approving overall direction and policy. *Stocks* are normally issued as either "preferred" or "common." In accounting, part of owner's equity. (See also *share.*)

storage (n)   That which is being kept for future use or implementation. In reference to computers, that part of the machine which holds data necessary for processing activities, most commonly on magnetic tape or disks.

store (v)   To hold or keep for future use.

strategy (n)   A comprehensive plan of action.

subsidiary (n)   A company that is controlled wholly or partially by another company (usually called the parent company). The parent has the dominant position because it owns or controls at least half of the stock in the *subsidiary* company.

suit (v)   To be appropriate or right for.

suitable (adj)   Appropriate for a specific purpose or activity.

supervision (n)   Direction and control of workers' performance by overseeing, teaching, and motivating.

support (v)   To provide the means for something to exist (e.g., to *support* research).

surplus (n)   The remainder, or balance, which accrues to any business organization (profit, nonprofit, or state-operated) when total liabilities (or costs) are subtracted from net assets; sometimes used in a socialistic economic system as the equivalent to profit in a capitalistic economic system. (See also *profit*.)

symbol (n)   A printed or written sign used to represent an operation, element, quantity, quality, or relationship (e.g., in computer programs and mathematics).

take place (v)   To occur; to happen.

target market (n)   An identified sales sector composed of the group of potential customers or consumers to whom a product(s) will be offered for sale.

task (n)   Unit of work or production that must be performed in accordance with one's job duties, usually assigned to an individual or group by a supervisor.

team (n)   A group working on the same project or task.

technical (adj)   Specialized; complex.

technology (n)   The application of science, especially to industrial or business objectives.

teleconferencing (n)   a way to enable people who are not in the same location to meet without the need for travel. A *teleconferencing* facility has video cameras, monitors, and a telephone network which allow people in different locations to see and talk to each other.

tend (v)   To be inclined in one way.

thus (adv)   Consequently; therefore.

time-sharing (n)   A method of dividing the total capacity of a computer into smaller units so that a number of users have regularly scheduled access for a predetermined amount of time.

tool (n)   Method, concept, or instrument that is needed to perform a task.

toward   In the direction of (e.g., to work *toward* an objective).

transaction (n)   Either a single piece of business or a group of goal-related business activities.

translate (v)   To express in another language, systematically retaining the original meaning.

turn to (v)   To go to (e.g., to *turn to* a supervisor for guidance).

unique (adj)   Being the only one of its kind; incomparable.

utilize (v)   To use for a specific purpose (e.g., *utilize* capital to start up a business).

valid (adj)   Based on true information; able to be supported by facts, statistics, etc.

valuation (n)   The established value or price of something.

variety (n)   A range; a number of different types.

vary (v)   To differ in form and substance.

view (v)   To see or look at; to survey.

vital (adj)   Very important; of critical importance.

weigh (v)   To consider; to evaluate.

whereas   On the other hand; while.

while   Although, even though.

wholesaler (n)   An individual or business acting as the intermediary or middleman in the distribution channel between the producer/manufacturer and the retailer. Generally sells in large quantities. (See also *channel of distribution* and *retailer*.)